Follow
Me
&
Leeds
United

Follow Me

Me

&

Leeds

United

Heidi Haigh

DB
PUBLISHING

This edition published in Great Britain in 2013 by DB Publishing, an imprint of JMD Media.

Copyright © Heidi Haigh 2013

The moral right of the author has been asserted

A catalogue record for this book is available from the British Library.

ISBN 9781780913087

Printed and bound by Copytech (UK) Limited, Peterborough.

Contents

This book is dedicated to my dad and mum, Fritz and Helga, Sue's dad and mum Eric and Nancy and family friend Arthur. Without their help, my dedicated support of Leeds United would never have happened

FOREWORD BY EDDIE GRAY

To me the lifeblood of any football club is the supporters. Without them there would be no football and it never ceases to amaze me the dedication they show to their respective football clubs.

The Author typifies the loyalty that fans show to their respective clubs. Heidi has travelled all over Europe watching her beloved club and knows first hand the humour and banter that flows from the terraces.

This book will remind Leeds United fans and supporters of other clubs of the ups and downs that befall most fans over the years. The highs and lows of following your beloved club are extreme, from ecstasy to despair.

Many Leeds United fans will appreciate the trials and tribulations our beloved club has suffered over the years. Unlike a lot of love affairs this one lasts forever. I think you will find this is a very entertaining read and something that most fans can relate to.

One of the most surprising things that happened to me when playing for Leeds United was winning the clubs first League Championship at Anfield in 1969. The reception we received from the home fans stunned us all. I must say that is not the norm in football but it goes to show that most fans appreciate quality when they see it.

Eddie Gray

PROLOGUE

I decided to write this book because when I started supporting Leeds United there weren't many women following football, especially away from home. The troubles my friends and I had to endure just to follow our team have been – especially in the seventies – harrowing and traumatic, coupled with some fantastic times. I also had seven years of never missing a match home and away including many European matches in the seventies. I lived in a village called Carlton, which is halfway between Goole and Selby so this book includes things that happened to me on my way to and from Leeds, which weren't always pleasant. It includes travelling to and from matches from Leeds, plus things that happened at different grounds during the match.

I am still as mad, passionate and loyal about Leeds United in 2013 as I was in the seventies and all times in between. I can still be found at Elland Road for every home match, noticeably still wearing a beret that is my trademark. I have always loved the singing and chanting and constantly lost my voice through being vociferous. Although the atmosphere now at Elland Road is nothing like it was in my earlier days of following Leeds, there have been some signs of it returning.

Sue and Carole (both staunch Leeds fans) and great friends of mine were going to contribute to this book, but I've written so much that this is all my own work. Our tales have taken us all over the country and all over Europe. We have been privileged to see the best team in the world throughout the Revie years. We have met thousands of Leeds fans over the years and the comeraderie we have is second to none. We have been through the highs and lows of being a Leeds fan, but we are still there following our team. Anyone who is a true fan will know that the love of your club is deep inside you. Not everyone can get to all the matches but once you are a Leeds fan you are always a Leeds fan.

There are a hard core of Leeds fans that come from Leeds but the majority have always come from outside the city. Seeing the different places displayed on the backs of the coaches, especially at away matches in the eighties, were an indication of the loyal and fanatical fans that Leeds United have.

Sue is my best friend from school. We met in the first year at Selby High School for girls (later the name changed to Selby Grammar School when it was amalgamated with Drax Grammar School for boys) and have stayed friends ever since. I can remember we were all sat in the classroom one dinnertime discussing who we supported and there were a few of us that were Leeds supporters.

Carole is another of my best friends and we met by going to all the away matches where we usually ended up on the same Wallace Arnold coach – mainly number one coach. Carole used to travel to matches with Margaret and they still sit together in the Kop at Leeds. I meet up with Sue and her husband Paul and Carole and her partner Ashley every home match. Sue is a home and away season ticket holder and hopefully one day I will get back to going to all the matches again, although I got to quite a few away matches last season. At the moment I am a home season ticket holder together with my two youngest daughters Danielle and Emily.

Although my eldest two children are Leeds supporters Jamie and Michelle don't go to many matches now due to cost although they did go to many matches, home and away, in their younger days. Michelle came to the last match of the season against Burnley in 2011 with her children, my two granddaughters Hannah then age three and Laura age one (even though their dad Steve is a Bradford City fan!) together with my niece Sonya. Who says women don't like football!!

All the family have been brought through the ranks correctly, follow Leeds and have been coming to matches from as young as six days old. Apart from my mum, (my dad is no longer with us) I have two sisters Karin and Erica and a brother Rolf, who are also Leeds United fans. Karen and Linda are other friends mentioned in the book, who I also met through travelling to away matches. There are many people who I met through my travels and whilst I don't remember everyone, there are a lot of people that still go to matches today.

Prologue

Throughout our European travels and some friendly matches, it was quite common to swap our scarves with the opposition fans. There were always lots of fans wanting us to do this and demand always outstripped the quantity, as we would only swap one scarf!

Many of these events were recorded with photographs and I have included a selection of them. Some of the photographs were copies I obtained from my friends including Sue, Carole, Margaret, Jonathan and Douggie. I have based the book on a diary I kept at the time and the memoirs are personal to me and are not meant to reflect on anyone in particular. In the early part of my diary I didn't really write a lot, but from the 1974–75 season I started writing more and going into more detail.

Although some things that happened were not good at the time, they are in the past and I never bore a grudge. I found that I always stuck up for Leeds fans no matter what happened and although I had a lot of trouble from certain Leeds fans they were in reality only a minority of people, though at the time I didn't see it that way. Gradually the attitude of many of these people who gave us grief changed when they saw that we continued to follow our team, although at the time I was the one out of my group of friends who received most of the abuse. In recent years it has been nice to see a shift in attitudes towards women and football although in the last couple of years I have seen this going backwards. We had a fantastic platonic relationship with many of our fans when I look back at things, as we all had the common cause of following and supporting our team Leeds United, which gave everyone a unique bond. Lots of our fans always made time to come and talk to us when they saw us and that was reciprocated by us. Also there may have been fall outs over the seasons (many a time it was drink involved) with my friends Sue, Carole, Karen and Linda (although the latter two don't go to matches at the moment), but we are all still the best of friends after all these years and I wouldn't have it any other way.

Chapter One

My Love Affair with Leeds United

My love affair with Leeds United began in 1965 with the FA Cup Final against Liverpool. Leeds United were the local team and we lost. The village where I lived, Carlton, also had links to Leeds United through a man named Brian Baker who ran a coach company from there, Abbey Coachways. Because he was also a Leeds supporter he put on coaches to travel to all Leeds United's home matches plus some away matches. What really consolidated my love of football was the 1966 World Cup. My mum and dad came from Germany so followed Germany through all the qualifying rounds; with the only match they missed being the Final. Mum kept the ticket stubs from the matches and also a World Cup Willie figure, which are now in my possession. We watched the final at home and were torn between following Germany and England because Jack Charlton was playing and he was a Leeds player!

I attended my first Leeds match in 1967 at the age of 12, when I went to Elland Road with my friend Sue and another friend Fiona. Sue's dad took us there for her birthday treat in August. I can't remember who we played or the score but at half time they played *Lily the Pink* by the Scaffold for us over the tannoy. We were over the moon when we heard our names read out. We stood near the front in Lowfields and this was how I became indoctrined into being a Leeds fan of over 45 years.

I didn't get to too many matches before I left school but I did go to the Inter-Cities Fairs Cup Finals against Ferencváros in 1968 and against Juventus in 1971 which Leeds won both times and we stood on Lowfields. At some point we changed from standing on Lowfields to standing on the open Kop called the Gelderd End. The cost to get in was two shillings and sixpence (2/6 or half a crown). Another match I can recall is when we played Liverpool and decided to go in the Scratching Shed and that was also the only time I ever went in there. The Scratching Shed was the stand where the Leeds fans congregated and most of the singing and chanting was done. It was the first time that I came across the stand being full because just as I got through the turnstiles with one of my friends the turnstiles clanked shut. Unfortunately my sister Karin was still outside and unable to get in. Luckily she managed to get into another part of the ground although I can't remember which part. All I can remember of the shed was that it was jam-packed and there was lots of singing. I think I managed to squeeze down to the front so I could see but memories are vague.

In 1971 when I left school at the age of 15, I started work immediately at Croda International, in Cowick; although Sue stayed on at school. We made a pact to see how many Leeds matches we could go to without missing one and to follow Leeds everywhere.

One of the next matches was Southampton away and to get there we would have had to get a coach from Leeds that left at 7.00 am on the morning of the match. Because of a lack of trains arriving on time in the morning it meant we would have had to go to Leeds the night before the match and have a long wait in Leeds station. I told my mum I was going to the match with Sue and ended up having an argument with her and wasn't allowed to go. I was very disappointed and vowed that I wouldn't back down next time. I was working and earning my own money so felt that I should be allowed to go.

I had got the bug of going to matches following my team, so when it came to the next away match which was Chelsea, I told my mum that I was going whether she liked it or not, so she conceded that I was going to the match. This was the start of a run of matches that I went to that spanned seven seasons of not missing a match home or away, plus I went to many away European matches. I was and still am very determined (stubborn even) when I set my mind to do something and once I decided I wasn't going to miss a match, I wasn't going to miss one! This could not have been done without the help of my parents though, especially my dad who took me by car to and from Leeds when going to far away matches. This was a good two-hour return trip for him each way as Leeds was approximately 30 miles away. Also a good family friend Arthur and Sue's dad helped out as well but for the majority of matches I depended on the input of my dad and I am eternally grateful.

A funny incident happened once when my dad and Arthur were parked up in the car waiting for Sue and me to return from an away match in the early hours of the morning. They were half asleep when a copper knocked on the window of the car and asked what they were doing there. My dad said I'm waiting for a girl, and then Arthur said no two girls. The copper asked what the registration number of the car was (it was NBR 521) but to remember it we had nicknamed the car 'never be ready at five to one', which is what my dad said to the copper. Then my dad said that they were waiting for us to come back from a Leeds match, which satisfied the curiosity of the copper. When we got back to the car from the coach, we couldn't stop laughing when they relayed this to us.

I never got involved in trouble because I was scared stiff, but something always seemed to happen around me. This was because I went to every match and many times there were not many of our fans in attendance wearing their colours like my friends and I. At Elland Road Leeds fans had the upper hand but away from home in the seventies there were only certain grounds where we took loads of fans. Some matches, there would only be one or two Wallace Arnold coaches going and you really took your life in your own hands. It wasn't until the late seventies when we started taking more and more fans away from home that Leeds fans started fighting back at these places.

The first away match I went to on my own was 29 January 1972, when I was 16. Sue couldn't go; she couldn't afford it with still being at school. I booked on a Wallace Arnold coach from Leeds, which meant I set off at 5.00 am from home to arrive in Leeds in plenty time for the coach at 7.00 am. This was a ritual for all the far away matches and it was a good job my dad was a farmer and used to early mornings. On arrival in Leeds I had to go to the Corn Exchange to get my ticket for the coach before going down to The Calls where the coaches departed from. I got a half fare to Tottenham on the coach and the total cost for the day was £2.10 including getting in to the match. The fact that I was travelling to a football match on my own didn't faze me. Once we arrived at the ground, I approached some women at the front of the coach and asked them if they minded me going in with them. This is how I met Chris, Colleen and Maureen. They were going into the unreserved seats and we ended up sat above the Tottenham fans behind the goal. A lad called Russ introduced himself to me on the way back on the coach so I had someone to talk to. I found it very easy to talk to Leeds fans and made friends very easily.

On 8 November 1972 my dad came to a match with us. This was because we were playing Carl Zeiss Jena in the European Cup Winners Cup in the second-round second leg. The only reason he wanted to go to it was because the team came from near where he was born in East Germany. The highlight for me was seeing Billy, Jack and a few other players walk past us outside the ground before the match. I was in my element; my heroes and I had seen them! My dad couldn't help but laugh at me, because I didn't even say hello to them, I was too star struck!

I found every close season torture without any football and I couldn't wait for the new season to start. It was great when there were friendlies either in this country or abroad before the start because it made the new season come round quicker.

At the beginning of the 1973–1974 season I started travelling in to Leeds on the train from Snaith, which called at Pontefract, Castleford and Woodlesford. Some of the local lads said I should travel in with them instead of going on Abbey Coachways, so this is what I started to do. It was quite a fitness regime in those days. I walked from Carlton to Snaith, walked from Leeds City Station to the ground and back again and then from Snaith to home. It never bothered me walking, although sometimes when it was dark it wasn't so nice and even though people would stop to offer me a lift I always declined. The more I travelled in on the Snaith train meant that I was starting to get recognised as a regular and a lad from Knottingley started calling me Leeds.

I often took my nephew and niece, Mark and Sonya to home matches with me, normally testimonials or friendlies. At Paul Madeley's testimonial I got skitted something cruel by loads of lads who thought Mark and Sonya were mine. This is how the next generation of Leeds fans are brought through the ranks; they are not allowed to support anyone else and are brought up following the right club! Normally when I went into the ground I got Mark and Sonya in for free, as the turnstile operators used to let them go through the turnstile at the same time as myself. I carried Sonya up the Kop as it was only a small crowd of 12,000 and I was asked if I'd brought my gang with me. Ian had brought his brother Mark with him and they stood with us whilst Mark and Sonya stood in the box at the back. Some of the Barnsley lads came and stood next to us and one gave Mark and Sonya 20p each.

I used to leave my coat in the Pools Office or the lockers at Leeds station because even if it was snowing and freezing cold I didn't wear a coat into the ground. When so many people were crammed together on the terraces you didn't need one, which wasn't normally a problem at home matches. Because I stood at the back of the Gelderd End you had to be in the ground by 1.00 pm otherwise you couldn't get up there as it was so packed. The only time I felt the cold was when going back to the station after the match as you certainly felt it then!!

10 August 1974 – the day before my birthday – took us to Wembley to see Leeds play in the Charity Shield against Liverpool. The score at the end of the match was 1–1 with Trevor Cherry scoring our goal. Billy Bremner got sent off for fighting with Kevin Keegan. The match ended up with penalties and David Harvey missed our fifth one, which meant Liverpool won the Charity Shield. Normally if the match was a draw both teams shared the shield with each club having it for six months each but that had changed this year. I still feel that if we had have done that, then we would have definitely won the European Cup at the end of the season, as things would have gotten off to a great start.

During the close season of 1975 I got engaged to Andy from Rotherham. Unfortunately this didn't last very long because once the season started I found I couldn't cope with his jealousy and the relationship ended. It all started at the Scarborough pre-season friendly; when a Leeds fan spoke to me I would always chat away and Andy thought a 'see you later' comment, meant that I was literally going to meet up with them, rather than it being a figure of speech. I am a very loyal person as I have shown following my team and I would never two-time anyone.

Whilst following Leeds, lots of things happened unexpectedly, which was all part and parcel of following them. For example breaking down on the way back from a night match at Arsenal. We didn't leave London until late because the coach only took us as far as Kings Cross and we had to find our own way to and from the ground. Luckily it was only a few stops to Highbury so it wasn't a bad journey on the tube. Unfortunately on the way home from London the coach got a puncture and we had to endure a long wait on the hard shoulder before we were able to continue on our way. We eventually arrived back in Leeds and the only way back home was to catch the milk train at approx 5.00 am. I eventually arrived home at 7.00 am and went straight to work at 8.00 am.

Another time I took half a day holiday off work and wasn't sure if the second leg of the League Cup semi-final match would be on, but after a pitch inspection at 2.30 pm I heard it was on so set off for Leeds in the car. The coach got to the Nottingham turn off of the motorway at 6.00 pm and the coppers stopped us and said the match was off. We were all mad when we had to turn round and go back to Leeds. In my eyes I had wasted a half day of my holidays because I saved them all for following Leeds.

Carole made me a Scotland banner for my Christmas present. We then started to get orders from Scotland and Leeds fans for them, so we ended up making, sewing and selling them. We also made badges for lads for the different areas that they came from, ie Carlton Whites, Snaith Whites etc. We saw Tony from Walsall and he and his friends paid for the badges we had made for them and we got £20 for them. The lads said we were walking sewing machines. This ensured that we could follow Leeds everywhere. Also at one time I had three jobs on the go at the same time, so that I could earn enough money to travel to every match and go abroad with Leeds.

Chapter Two

Fame & Fortune

My first claim to fame came on *Match of the Day* on 1 April 1972 when I went to Derby County and stood right by the corner flag next to the Pop Side where the away fans stood. That evening I was thrilled to see myself on the television when Leeds took a corner. After the match I saw the players come out to the team coach and patted Norman, Peter, Billy and Gary on their backs.

The first match of the season on 12 August 1972 saw Leeds take on Chelsea at Stamford Bridge. Before we set off from The Calls on a Wallace Arnold coach, a group of us, Joan, Maureen, Esther, Chris, Colleen and me had our photo taken, which was on the front page of the *Yorkshire Evening Post*. The day didn't end very well as Leeds started disastrously getting beaten 4–0.

The FA Cup fourth-round against Peterborough on 26 January 1974 saw the photographer from the *Yorkshire Evening Post* again take a photo of Sue and me. This was taken whilst we were waiting for the coaches at The Calls and ended up on the front page of the paper. Leeds took 8,000 fans to this fixture where there was lots of fighting and our fans smashed a hut. Before the next home match Sue and I went to the *Evening Post* building on Wellington Street to get a copy of our picture.

Travelling to Bristol City in the FA Cup fifth-round in February 1974 saw Sue and I get recognised by some Leeds lads who had seen our picture in the paper. By going to all the matches I was starting to recognise a lot of people and was forever talking to lots of Leeds fans. People were also starting to recognise us and always made time to talk to us.

When I won a trip to the World Cup in 1974 as a pools agent for Leeds United, I ended up being in the local papers in Goole and Selby. I had to show I was a Leeds fan and wore my scarf and a badge for the photos.

I was often asked who I supported by some Leeds fans, as I was dressed like a 'Christmas tree'! I like wearing my colours to show I support Leeds United (even now I am constantly wearing my Leeds shirt in Halifax where I live). As the seasons progressed I wore many scarves at the same time, mostly tied around my wrists, and/or one round my neck. In Barcelona for the European Cup semi-final in 1975 I wore seven scarves, three round one wrist, two round the other, one round my neck and one tied round my head. Once I was getting recognised lads also called me a part timer, although they knew I went to all the matches because they'd seen me there. This was evident whilst we were queuing to get in to the ground at Liverpool when the Donny and Whitley lads arrived and we were all shouting to each other. Wherever you went we all acknowledged each other, because you recognised faces and there was always a hardcore of people who went to every match like me.

Unfortunately, because I wore my colours it felt like trouble followed me around everywhere. When I arrived at Leeds station I saw a Leeds fan from Derby who asked if I had gone to the Ipswich match and then said that he had seen me there. This was happening more and more and because my name was unusual I often had my name shouted out. I always remembered faces; unfortunately I was not brilliant at remembering the names of our fans, although obviously I remembered the names of ones who we travelled with regularly. In the Gelderd End we had the lads from York behind us who kept nipping us and talking about our photo being in the paper.

When lots of our fans were around I felt safe even when they were fighting. I was always grateful when they were there because it meant they would hopefully stop any opposing fans from getting me, especially as trouble kept following me around.

We played Wimbledon in a rearranged match that took place at Selhurst Park, the home of Crystal Palace. Again there were loads of Leeds fans there. I was asked if I came from Leeds and someone else told them I came from Goole. Carole ended up getting pushed down the terraces, which ripped her trousers and she wasn't happy! We were in our element in the ground because we couldn't believe the posh ladies loos at Selhurst Park. There were pink tiles on the wall and mirrors above the basins. After the horrendous conditions of most of the ladies toilets at football grounds these were the height of luxury. At the end of the match we saw the team off and I patted Billy Bremner and Joe Jordan on the back. Frank Gray waved at us and Eddie Gray smiled at us. This was another match where I got back home at 6.30 am, stayed up and went straight to work at 8.00 am.

On 6 September 1975 before the Wolves match at Elland Road we had our pictures taken in the West Stand car park by the *Daily Express* (Sue, Carole, Linda and I) with a crowd of fans watching this happen. Carole had written a letter to them expressing how we tried to keep out of trouble by going on the service train but the coppers were adamant we had to go on the football special trains, but we had refused. These trains were put on specifically to take football fans to away matches, sometimes more than one depending on the number of fans that were going to the match. We had been on these trains previously, but we had decided that we wanted to stay out of any trouble and would find our own way to matches. We were being treated like fourth-class citizens just because we wear football club scarves and are young girls. The following week our pictures were in the *Evening Post*.

On 13 September 1975 we went to Stoke where we lost 3–2 with Lorimer scoring both our goals. Whilst we were on Selby station, an old man I knew from Carlton asked if we'd seen ourselves in the *Daily Express*. We hadn't so we bought a paper. In Leeds we went to Terry Cooper's shop and showed them the paper and they said 'fame at last'. We travelled to the match on Wallace Arnold coaches. Violet was on coach two and some lads we'd seen at Sheffield pointed to us. Got in the ground and some lads said they had seen me in the paper. When we got to the top of the steps some more shouted, 'it's the *Daily Express* girls!' We went down to the toilets at the bottom of the terraces with the Leeds fans chanting *Daily Express* to us. When leaving the coach park a fella in the coach behind us held up a copy of the *Daily Express* and pointed to our picture; although embarrassed, we did wave at all the Leeds fans. Saw the Donny coach opposite ours and some of them kept looking at us. Our letter was in the *Green Post*. Later whenever lads saw us they were always saying it's the *Daily Express* girls.

March 1976 saw the visit of Arsenal to Elland Road. At the ground Sue, Carole and I went into the Pools Office, then the club shop and all these Japanese who had come to see Leeds started taking photos of us. Every time we tried moving away another one of them came up and asked us to stop for a photo. We went into the Peacock, spoke to the Kettering lads and some more Japanese took our photos again. As I got onto the station a lad grabbed my arm and said "you went to Wolves with us and used to wear a bib and brace (my dungarees) with badges on." As I went onto the platform some more Japanese took photos of us and a fella grabbed my train ticket from me and read off it, "Queen of the fans".

Travelling on Wallace Arnold, Mick Barker a Rangers fan from Seacroft was on about the Rank Xerox fella who came to where I worked at Croda to mend the photocopier. He had told Mick all about me and how he had come across this lass who went everywhere following Leeds. It's funny how we ended up travelling on the same coach. Talking to Phil and Chris and a lad went past and said "hello Heidi". Phil said, "You'd think you lived here, what's it like to be famous?"

In April 1977 we ended up in the paper again. I went to pick Carole up and she said, "we're in the *Daily Express* with the headlines We're Terrified". Prior to playing man utd at Hillsborough in the FA Cup semi-final on 23 April, Carole had written another letter to them complaining about man utd supporters being given tickets in our end at Hillsborough and the amount of trouble that it would cause. Their fans had just been involved in a lot of trouble at Norwich where they had wrecked the ground. Also Sue had stopped going to most matches by this time because of all the trouble at them. Carole was sat talking to Mac, Tony, Reeder, Douggie and others in the club. As soon as I walked up they started on about the letter and said we'd made Leeds fans out to be cowards and we said, "No way, the only ones that are cowards are us three (Carole, Sue and I), as trouble was following us everywhere and we were scared." This time we had a lot of our fans having a go at us for this article saying they weren't scared of man utd. It didn't say that; there were only our three names there and no mention of anyone else.

At the beginning of the 1977 season, a group of fans including myself were asked by John in the Pools Office if we would form the Kop Committee.

The Committee consisted of Leeds fans that travelled everywhere and John had asked us to join, to promote Peter Lorimer's Testimonial year and help with events. Before Leeds took on Birmingham City at Elland Road on 27 August we had to try and sell the *'Kop's Night Out'* tickets for Peter Lorimer's Testimonial and found it was hard going. We saw the lad from Halifax with the white shirt that I had taken photos of in Belgium in 1977 and he kissed my hand (I ended up marrying him in 1988). We also had to go back into the ground and have our photos taken before the match on the pitch as we were the Kop Committee. Not all the Committee were there and they said they couldn't wait for the rest of them to arrive and took the photo. As I was going back into the Kop one said, "It's her who had her photo taken – come in number nine" and some others said "It's her" and cheered. This picture ended up in a supporter's magazine in later years with someone saying that Princess Diana was a Leeds fan (with an arrow pointed at me) and that I looked like her as I had a similar hairstyle.

On Saturday 24 September 1977 Leeds were at home to man utd and after the match was the *'Kop's Night Out'*. After the match I went to the Queens Hall and dumped my case upstairs and then went to sit in the office at the front to take tickets. One of the bouncers said, "So you're Heidi, pleased to meet you". I saw loads coming in who I knew and I'd taken 150 tickets before I came off the desk. Trevor Cherry came in and said, "I don't need a ticket do I?" so I said, "No I'll let you off". I went to get changed but as I got to the squash club they said that they wanted us for a photo and had to stay in our gear. Went into the club and Peter Lorimer, Gordon McQueen, Joe Jordan, Trevor Cherry and Tony Currie were there plus Alan from Morecambe, Eric Carlile and a Scottish lad too. I was knocking a few drinks back before we had a photo taken. The team went to give autographs and then all went. I said to Joe. "Did you enjoy the match?" and he said, "Yes, did you?" Gordon said the same to Carole. I asked Peter if he knew how we could get tickets for the Wales match and was talking to him about Scotland and he said he wanted them for his testimonial. I said that he must be telepathic because I'd only said that last week because they'd bring some fans. Got changed and later had a photo taken with Peter Lorimer. No one would believe that it was us (I'd got my blue dress on) and they said we'd both got a pair of legs and how nice we looked.

They said I should wear a dress more often, especially to matches. I don't think so!! I couldn't stop giggling before falling on the floor. I don't know why but everyone was saying how drunk I was! Steve from Shipley saw me back to the station and I started being sick and was all the way to the train. On the train I fell asleep and woke up with Dickie from Selby sat next to me. Dad picked me up in Selby and I was sick at home and woke up the next day with a massive hangover and was still being sick. I didn't recover properly until Monday.

Before home matches we normally went into the Leeds United Supporters Club located on Fullerton Park just off Elland Road. Part of the club was a social club and to get in there you had to be a member. These cards were checked on entrance and we always had a run in with a man called Pigeon who was on the door. At this time we always wore our scarves round our wrists like many of our fans. Unfortunately Pigeon didn't like us wearing them like this as, 'we were hooligans'. He always made us take them off before we could go in and it used to annoy us greatly as we weren't doing anything wrong by wearing our scarves. We had never done anything either to warrant being looked at as hooligans. One time as we went into the Supporters Club to renew our membership cards we had a run in with him. He told us to take our scarves off our wrists and I tried to say we would only be a minute, to which I was told if I was arguing the door was over there. I needed the card to get into opposition supporters clubs otherwise I wouldn't have bothered going in because he was a right pain. It was getting like a prison to support your team. Carole had a do with him once when he said we weren't allowed to go in and out of the Supporters Club all the time. Then I got told to take my scarves off my wrists but I could wear them round my belt. There were probably only a few times when he smiled and said hello to me and then I wondered what I had done to change his opinion of us.

Because of all the problems we had with Pigeon I wrote a letter to Mike Lockwood at the club complaining about him. In February 1976 a group of us made the long trip to Celtic for a friendly and when we went down to their Supporters Club, found our Supporters Club lot were there on a big coach half full! We'd been told it was full and Carole and I weren't going to be allowed on under any circumstances. Unfortunately by complaining it meant that we were told no coaches were running to the friendly. Well it didn't stop us from going to the match because we travelled up by train instead and had a great time anyway.

Kevin Sharpe played cricket for Yorkshire and was a close friend of ours along with his friend Bob Vasey. We met whilst travelling on Wallace Arnold coaches to away matches. When Kevin was going on a tour to Australia with Yorkshire, he had a leaving do at Meanwood that we were invited to. After the party we met his parents and brother at their house and we had a good talk to them. Kevin's mum told me to look after him at the match especially as Bob was being a right stirrer telling them all sorts of things. She also said she'd be worried to death whilst he was in Oz.

I missed my first match in years at Arsenal on 10 December 1977 because I was having my tonsils out. Too much shouting and singing at football matches meant I kept losing my voice. The lads reckoned I was going to have a baby and I should breathe out. Ruth teased me saying I was a part-timer and a lad told me that I was a great supporter. Saw Gary Edwards and Gary Noble who said they'd heard that I wasn't going to Arsenal and that if you miss that one you're going to miss a lot more. I said I'd rather miss one match than loads and Tony said we'll see you back with a bouncing boy and we'll send you a get well card.

Later, I was stood with Andy and others from Selby in Leeds station and we ended up talking to some QPR fans. They said Sally (a Leeds fan from London) looked a trouble maker and also that we were mad up here for wearing scarves, patches etc because in London they hardly wear anything. I said it shows how fanatical Leeds fans are and if it wasn't for folk coming from out of Leeds to support them they wouldn't have much support because they're fickle in Leeds. There are a hardcore of fans from the city but not as many as there should be. Sally said to them that they don't wear patches on their scarves because they nip over to Chelsea. One lad said that they don't hit lasses and Chelsea gets all their support as only 90 came up from London. Caught the train and had Andy and Colin going on about tonsils. Andy said to the guard have you any first aid on here because she's going to have a baby any minute? I was in hysterics and laughing so much my stomach hurt and they said quick get the guard. After I'd had my tonsils out Mick and Andy from Selby and loads of others kept telling me to speak louder when all I could do was whisper!

Whilst travelling to West Bromwich at the end of December 1977 on a coach hired by Ian, the Meanwood lads were sat on the back seat and they kept making comments. We got so far along the road and us girls were sat in our seats when all of a sudden came a chorus from the Meanwood lot at the back of, 'we all agree Heidi's tits are magic'. I could have died with embarrassment and then they kept singing things about them; my breasts and they were going to do things to me and have a gangbang. I went bright pink especially as they kept the songs up until Birmingham. On the coach on the way back they started singing again and I went to sort them out and hit Bob as he was the nearest and they kept trying to pull me onto the back seat. Just as we were getting back into Leeds they decided they wanted to kiss Peter Lorimer on my T-shirt and then nearly dragged it off my back. Everyone thought it was funny and I said they were disgusting. They decided I'd enjoyed it because I'd been talking to them and I was only trying to stick up for myself.

Two days later we played Newcastle at Elland Road. I was just watching the match generally in the first half and it went deathly silent and all of a sudden came a grand chorus ever so loud of the dreaded chant 'We all agree Heidi's t*ts are magic' and then Meanwood. I screamed, went bright pink and could have crawled under a stone. One lad told me to move my arms so he could see. It got to half-time and I went down with Ruth and Brian and a lad shouted at me. I saw Mick from Selby and he said something, then saw Robbie from Goole and he hugged me and said, "Is it you they're singing about?"

I got down to the bottom of the steps and Ian and Steve were there and they started laughing at me, so I told them to shut up, they'd planned it and waited till it was quiet to sing it. Went back up with Ian leading the way and he took us to where the Meanwood lot were and before I got there a lad said, "Yes Heidi's t*ts are magic" and Ian nudged them so they all started singing again and I dived into them. Again at the next match the inevitable chant went up and when I went downstairs at half-time saw Arnold so I dived on him, grabbed his scarf and as he turned round called him a swine. With that they all cheered, said, "This is Heidi" and I got dived on. They all asked if I was going to stand with them and I said no I was going down. As I went under the barrier I got attacked again and had my bum grabbed. As I was fighting with these to get past got grabbed again and had everyone staring but I managed to get to the bottom of the Kop. I saw a Welsh lad there who said, "How is it everyone knows you?" and I said, "It was because I was such a good Leeds fan." Mick Whiteley shouted we've heard them singing about you and so did Carole and Sue as they'd heard it where they stood and it was really clear. Got downstairs and Schulz said the same. Saw Ian so he led the way back up the Kop with Ruth and me following and people kept grabbing my bum and staring. I then got attacked all round and I thought I'd end up getting raped so I just lashed out at anyone. I was dived on before I got under the barrier and Brian and some others said, "Stay here we'll look after you." I was absolutely wacked and I'd no energy left to argue. Later a lad said, "Hello Heidi, see you," and then shouted "they're magic Heidi" and put his thumbs up and I said "I know they are" and he said, "Leeds as well." I could have killed him because I'd put my foot right in it as I thought he meant Leeds but he meant t*ts. Back in the Supporters Club as I went to the bar for a drink two lads were sat down and they started on about the song about me and one said "I don't agree really" and I said "I don't either." The next home match saw Mark Gallagher say to this lad, "This is Heidi who they sing about on the Kop."

At every home match I bought my programmes from the same seller and I always went to see the same badge seller. They were always giving me compliments and saying that I had lost weight. One said, "Where's your hubby, does he come as well or do you leave him at home?" I said I wasn't married to which the reply was, "come off it". I said, "I am not as I've better things to do". He said "Such as?" and I said "Coming to football matches". I couldn't understand why anyone would think I was married or even had a boyfriend for that matter.

In March 1978 we travelled to Liverpool by car and then walked down to Liverpool's Supporters Club and met John Green the committee member who we'd made a Scotland banner for and he bought Carole and me a coke. I said we were going in the Anfield Kop to watch the match and they said we'd be okay where they stood so Carole, Sue and I went in with them We ended up right in the middle about half way up behind the goal and stood with the lads and their mates. They told them we were Leeds fans and that's when I started panicking because I wondered what would happen to us if we scored. As it was we didn't because Liverpool scored as Leeds lost 1–0 but the lads were great and we were talking to one of the lads and he was ever so nice. Whilst I was talking to him about grounds, trouble, winning trips and me selling bingo cards, a fella turned round and asked if I had any League Cup final tickets but I hadn't. As we got out of the Kop I lost Sue and Carole but I couldn't stop grinning to myself because I thought what would the Liverpool fans think if they knew I was a Leeds fan? After we'd gone John Green invited Barry and the others back to his house for tea which I think was a great gesture and I wish all fans were like him and the others we met. As it was when we stopped at the services on the way back the Fullerton Park coach was in. Phil said there'd been a lot of trouble by the coaches and three lads on their coach had been attacked and one had his programmes pinched. We put the Leeds stickers back in the car windows.

At a Leicester City match we got near the ground and saw the Shrewsbury lot who couldn't get in any pub. We decided to carry on and went down to the pub and the bouncer on the door nodded that we could go in, Carole, Steve, Mick and I. As we walked in a lad pointed at me, they all cheered and clapped me and shouted get 'em off and I went bright pink. It was the Halifax lads and Bob Vasey. I went to the toilets and one of the Birmingham lasses said she'd heard the reception I got when I walked into the pub. There was a fantastic atmosphere there with everyone singing which was great. At half-time I went to the loo and found all the Leeds lads were using the girls' toilets. I wouldn't go in at first till I was sure they had all come out then saw Sheena and Joyce so went in. When I came out I saw Fiona and told her I'd stand guard so I threatened any lad who tried to get in.

At Leeds I went to the bar in the Supporters Club and as I was stood there an old fella came up and said, "Wasn't I speaking?" I said could he tell me where I knew him from as I couldn't remember and he asked if I knew this other fella and I remembered then that I'd met them on the plane to Salonika. I said, "It was you who got me drunk," and he said. "I got them drunk." Went to see Margaret and the old fella went past and said that he got arrested in Paris.

Left: FA Cup 26th January
1974. Sue and Heidi
- autographed on the
back by team (courtesy
Yorkshire Evening Post –
Peterborough)

Below: 1975 – Sue, Heidi,
Linda and Carole (courtesy
Daily Express)

Kop Committee Peter Lorimer Testimonial (courtesy Yorkshire Evening Post)

Kop Committee Barry, Heidi, Sharon, June, Mick (courtesy Yorkshire Evening Post)

Chapter Three

Don Revie and Brian Clough

Don Revie was in charge of the best team that I had the privilege of seeing play. Sprake, Reaney, Cooper, Bremner, Charlton, Hunter, Lorimer, Clarke, Jones, Giles, Gray with substitute Madeley, are names that are revered around the world. They are also the names of the players I thought were Leeds United at their best. It was Don and the team's legacy that brought about my loyalty and unswerved support of Leeds United. It is because of this team that I ended up travelling all over the country and the world to see them. I used to think in the seventies what would happen when the team broke up, would I still support Leeds? The truth is Leeds United captured my heart along with many others and is in my blood.

Under Don Revie's management Leeds United won the English League Championship twice in 1969 and 1974 and finished runners-up in five other seasons. They won the FA Cup in 1972 and went to Wembley on three other occasions in 1965, 1970 and 1973. They won the League Cup in 1968 and the Inter-Cities Fairs Cup in 1968 and 1971. They were European Cup Winners' Cup Finalists in 1973 and European Cup Finalists in 1975. They were one of the most successful teams of the era.

Most other fans hated Leeds United as a team, wherever we went. The media always portrayed Leeds as dirty and if ever there was anything involving Leeds fans then they would go into overdrive to report it. As far as I am concerned, Leeds players were no dirtier than for example Harris at Chelsea and Smith at Liverpool to name a couple. We were a hard team and played to win and there is nothing wrong with that. We were successful and without many dubious and bribed refereeing decisions, which were proven, we would have gained more trophies.

I also feel that Don Revie did not get the recognition he deserved for giving myself and thousands of others, the privilege of seeing the best team ever seen play. Fundraising efforts culminated with a statue of Don Revie being put up at Elland Road in recognition of his efforts and achievements with Leeds United. This has been long overdue. As soon as I heard about the fund raising, I had to go to these events to support them, as Don Revie and his Leeds United team were and still are part of my life. These events were supported by the team players from his time as manager of Leeds and the rapport we had with these players is still evidenced whenever we see them. They also still refer to Don Revie as 'the gaffer'.

Don Revie treated his players like family and looked after them well. He also ensured that the players gave something back to the fans by attending the annual function at Menwith Hill near Harrogate. Training sessions used to be held on Fullerton Park opposite the West Stand. Fans used to be able to stand at the perimeter fence and watch them train before getting their autographs and taking pictures. The team used to train in a morning before going across to Sheila's café on Elland Road where they ate and relaxed in the back room.

Don Revie also had a great relationship with Bill Shankly the manager of Liverpool. They were forever ringing each other up and had the greatest respect for each other. It was fitting that when Leeds United won their first ever League Championship in 1969 that they won it at Anfield, Liverpool. Although I wasn't there that night, I was told that Billy Bremner took the lads over to the Liverpool Kop who chanted 'Champions' to them.

Leeds were leading in the 1970 Cup Final against Chelsea, which was being shown on the television. Leeds looked as if they were going to win the FA Cup for the first time in their history under Don Revie when Sprake the goalkeeper made an error. The ball slipped through his hands for them to equalise and it meant that Chelsea forced a replay.

The 1971–1972 season culminated with some of the finest displays that I've ever seen from a Leeds United team. On 19 February 1972 we beat man utd (this is a swear word as far as I am concerned but is in lower case for the purpose of this book) 5–1 with Jones getting a hat trick and Clarke and Lorimer getting the others. On 4 March 1972 came the 7–0 drubbing of Southampton. This was also the first match that Sue and I went and stood at the top of the Kop in the middle behind the goal. The way Leeds tortured Southampton with the finest display ever seen by our team was a privilege to see. At the start of 1972 Leeds progressed well in the FA Cup and then won the semi-final at Hillsborough, which ended with Leeds getting to Wembley in our Centenary Year. We arrived late due to getting stuck in traffic. It just felt right and justified when we beat Birmingham City 3–0 and I knew we were going to Wembley. I sent off for my ticket by cutting out all the tokens from my programmes and was ecstatic when I received my ticket.

The FA Cup Final on 6 May 1972 was the first big match away from home that I attended. To be going to the Final was a dream come true. I travelled down with Abbey Coachways to the Final with Sue, her mum, dad and brother Phillip and another friend Janet Milner from Selby. My recollection of Wembley that day was of an awesome stadium and it being a privilege to be there. I was behind the goal where the players came out and to the left of the tunnel. Singing *Abide With Me* was fantastic and it still remains one of my favourite hymns to this day. Tommy Steele who was leading the singing came out wearing white so the Leeds fans sang Tommy's wearing white (meaning he was supporting us). The singing of the National Anthem prior to the start of the match was an awesome and inspiring scene, with the whole stadium of fans singing in unison, which was a fantastic sight to see. The Leeds fans were in fantastic form singing throughout the pre-match entertainment and during the match. It's funny but I just knew we were going to win it, although until the final whistle went there were some worries that Arsenal would get back into it. When Allan Clarke scored the goal we were dancing and crying with joy. The only thing that really went wrong was when Mick Jones went down, dislocated his elbow and was in so much pain.

When the final whistle blew and we knew we had won the Cup, the feelings were out of this world. The fans that haven't experienced us winning anything – but only the disappointments – have really missed out on the experience. To then see Billy go up the steps to lift the FA Cup from Her Majesty the Queen was a joy to behold!!! I was crying with happiness but then sadness when Mick went up with Norman Hunter to receive his medal. On the coach pulling away from Wembley a can of beer was thrown at the window by Arsenal fans. This hit the window next to us and someone shouted at me to take my banner down from the window. I did this reluctantly but that was the only bit of violence I saw that day.

On to the following Monday night, 8 May 1972, Leeds were forced to play their last match of the season at Wolverhampton, two days after the FA Cup Final. This should have been played at least on the Wednesday to give the team time to recover from the match but no such grace was given. Leeds had requested a postponement because they were trying to win the double, the FA Cup and the League. I had no holidays to take at work so asked if I could have three days off without pay. In those days you had to work for a while before being entitled to take any holidays with pay. By doing this it enabled me to get to the match and I travelled with Abbey Coachways. When we arrived at Wolverhampton there were thousands of Leeds fans there and coaches galore. Sue and I made our way to the turnstiles and the queues were immense. We queue jumped and just seemed to get down to near the front of the queues as we were so little and female, but people let us in. I think that was the only way we got in before the turnstiles were closed and it meant we were lucky because at least 10,000 fans were locked outside the ground. We stood halfway up the stand and everyone around us seemed taller and with the amount of people stood in front of us on the terraces, we could only see the far side of the pitch from the halfway line. We could have tried to get nearer the front but the crowd was jam-packed. Wolves beat Leeds 2–1 and from my point of view this was the first match that we were robbed. When you see their players playing pat a ball in the penalty area not once but twice, which should have been penalties and umpteen challenges going amiss you realise that the ref is going to give you nothing. It certainly felt like the powers that be were determined we would get nothing. I didn't see Billy's goal until next day on the TV and because I got so upset my mum said that I shouldn't go anymore! Well of course I never did, did I? By now Leeds was in my blood and there was no way I was missing any matches!

We actually did end up with the 'double' this year when we went on to win the West Riding Cup against Halifax Town when we beat them 4–3 at Elland Road. Peter Lorimer scored a hat trick, with one goal scored from the half way line.

We returned to Wembley to play Sunderland in the 1973 FA Cup Final. When we were there against Arsenal I knew we would win the cup, this year it felt different and it was because we lost. I was upset to see groups of Sunderland fans in with us at the tunnel end and all wearing their colours. Apparently some Leeds season ticket holders had sold their tickets to Sunderland fans and I was disgusted to find them in with us. I couldn't believe anyone would sell his or her tickets to the opposition fans!

The first match of the season on 25 August 1973 was at home to Everton and we won 3–1 with goals from Bremner, Giles and Jones. This season was to be the best season of watching Leeds and I was there to share the glories. It was also the start of a 29-match unbeaten run, which saw the superstitions that Don Revie had, become part of our lives. For instance my Leeds scarf remained unwashed throughout our unbeaten run, because to wash it would have meant us losing a match! It also meant that at the end of the season Leeds were crowned League Champions again and Don was to leave Leeds on a high.

At the end of the 1973–1974 season I felt this was a bad time for Leeds because Don Revie announced he was leaving to manage the England team. I didn't want him to go as he was part of Leeds but I could understand that he didn't want to be the one who broke the Leeds team up, as some of the players were nearing the end of their careers. Don had recommended Johnny Giles to the board as the next manager but for some reason the board decided against this. If they had appointed from within the club, continuity would have reigned and who knows how successful Leeds would have continued to be. As it was this meant that at the start of the 1974–1975 season we had the misfortune of being saddled with a manager who hated us, namely Brian Clough. I hated this appointment from the word go because of all the things he had previously said about Leeds publicly, which weren't very nice. I couldn't understand why he had been appointed manager in the first place. I was down at Elland Road with Sue when they made the appointment as I was off work because I had damaged my coccyx (that happened when I was reading a newspaper report about Leeds and sat down on the corner of the chair back. The pain was excruciating!) We were outside the Pools Office when Yorkshire Television came and interviewed us. They asked us whether we thought Clough was a good choice and we both said no. When asked again I said, "He had too big a mouth." I can remember watching this later on at Margaret's house and seeing myself on the television was a great thrill. Unfortunately I came in for a grilling from work because I had been at Leeds and seen on TV, but as my job was a sitting down one I managed to explain it away.

Whilst in Zurich on 2 October 1974 for the European Cup match we found out that Brian Clough had been sacked, how we cheered. Sue and I had agreed before the match that this was to be our last Leeds match ever, whilst Clough was in charge and wanted to 'push him out of the aeroplane'. Obviously this wasn't going to happen, because we weren't even on the same plane, but were being dramatic anyway. We waited for the team to come out of the players' entrance after the match. Sue and I chased after Manny Cussins, the Chairman of Leeds at the time and asked him whether we could be manager and his reply was that of course we could so we were thrilled with his comments.

Unfortunately when we got back to England the next day we found out that Manny Cussins had appointed Jimmy Armfield as manager. We were disappointed not to have been appointed but we got the best manager after Don Revie. Armfield was a real gentleman and someone who always had time for us fans. We also went to look round the ground with another Leeds fan that had been to Zurich on our trip. Whilst we were waiting to enter the ground from the West Stand we had the privilege of seeing Duncan McKenzie doing his party piece for the first time. We watched as he took a run and then jumped straight over a mini car. It was amazing to see this first hand and this was also witnessed by his team mates.

Leeds fans sang, "Hey rock and roll, Cloughies on the dole," at the next home match, which sounded brilliant and we thought it was excellent. We were glad to see the back of him and couldn't have been happier. As far as I am aware the majority of Leeds fans shared the feelings.

Before the players left Leeds for the European Cup Final against Bayern Munich in Paris in 1975, a Don Revie XI team came to play in Norman Hunter's testimonial at Elland Road. Even though Don was manager of England and not Leeds he still attended the European Cup Final. Jimmy Armfield also respected Don's team and gave the places in the side for the final to them, as this was their last chance to win the cup. Some fans think that he shouldn't have done that but if it hadn't have been for the referee allegedly being bribed, then I am positive that we would have won the cup with them instead of losing 2-0.

Don Revie was later to contract Motor Neurone, a muscle wasting disease, which was incurable. A benefit match was arranged in 1988 in aid of Motor Neurone Disease and I think that was one of the last times Don visited Elland Road before his death the following year. Billy Bremner was manager of Leeds at the time and the majority of Don's team were in attendance. Over 7,000 of us attended the match including my husband, two young children Jamie and Michelle and myself. It was very moving seeing the television reports after the event, when I saw how the disease had affected Don who was in a wheelchair at this time and struggled to speak. His memory will always be part of Leeds United.

Chapter Four

Coppers & Lads treatment of girls

at football matches

The East Midlands was always a bad place for Leeds fans to go to, as the coppers didn't like them. A match at Leicester City in February 1973 was very bad for Leeds fans as I saw that the Leicester coppers were arresting many of them for no reason at all. Likewise in the West Midlands at Coventry the following year the coppers were being very brutal with the Leeds fans although not me personally.

On 30 August 1975 we went on the special train to Sheffield United. The coppers were awful, treating all lads and lasses the same. We had queued up at the Shoreham stand again where they let so many Leeds fans in and then stopped the rest of us, herding us to the away end and Carole ended up with a horse standing on her foot. The Leeds fans in their end had a torrid time with fighting all over. Rob a very quiet lad was beaten up by the coppers in our stand and dragged out of the ground when he didn't do anything wrong. We acted as witnesses for him later when he had to go to court. I was crushed in the special queue whilst waiting at Sheffield station and had to put up with some wandering hands before I managed to get out of the way. Gary Noble had a go at some lads for calling us names. At least someone stuck up for us and showed not all lads were bad.

I took my nephew Mark with me to a match at Elland Road. Because Mark was so little I used to take him up to the back of the Kop and stand him in the boxes where the coppers stood so that he could see. One time Mark suddenly started to run off so I started to chase after him to catch him. A copper suddenly grabbed me by the hair and nearly pulled it out. When I pointed out my nephew he let me go but there was no need for that sort of treatment.

Sometimes we had a good laugh with coppers at away matches. On arrival at many grounds the coppers were always waiting to search the fans before they were allowed in. One thing male coppers weren't allowed to do was search us girls. More often than not in the early days of following Leeds there weren't many female coppers about. Because of this whenever we saw the lads being searched I would say to the coppers that they couldn't search me because I was female. They often joked that they could but I would scream and run past them whilst they were laughing their heads off. At least it showed that some had a sense of humour and it was nice to see them in a different light. On arrival at Coventry we all walked round to their end. The coppers were stopping all the lads and searching them and one said, "Come on lads over here." I didn't realise he had said it at first but then said, "I'm not a lad", to which I got the reply "what about equality?" I said, "Not in this case there isn't." As we got to where the lads were being searched I told the coppers to keep their hands off me and one made a move towards me so I screamed and ran through them very quickly. These lads were laughing their heads off at us as well. We got in the boys' entrance and Ian and Gary had to pay full. They were complaining that we shouldn't be going in the boys' entrance because we were too old. Unfortunately we had the last laugh because no one believed them! The following year at Coventry we weren't allowed in their end. We got round to the open end and I said to the coppers that they couldn't search me and one said, "Would you like to bet." I said, "You can search my scarves and that's all" and he let me through. In the ground there was fighting with the coppers and a running rampage. At a different match at Derby, there were loads of Leeds fans and coaches. We all got searched as we got off the coaches and we had two women coppers waiting for us. A copper and our driver wanted to search me and I told them to get lost. When we did get searched by female coppers all the lads liked to stop, watch and cheer.

My friends normally met me in Leeds station and we always went into town first. Unfortunately the coppers were always waiting in the station and told us that they couldn't let us into town. They said we could only go if we took all our Leeds things off – yes great seeing as we were covered in Leeds things as usual and I would be down to my underwear. I don't think so. After an argument with the coppers they let us across to the Scarborough pub. They said lasses were as bad as the lads and we were all nutters. Another time I met Carole and Sue outside the station as they had been chucked out of there, as the coppers didn't like Leeds fans hanging around the station.

After one match we had got back to the station and went across to the shop and were discussing how long the queue was and this inspector came up to us and said, "Come along either get on the platform or get off the station." Then he said, "What are you going to do?" We made to move off and he grabbed my arm and said, "Make your mind up or I'll arrest you." I was flabbergasted and said I had to get my train ticket first but he wouldn't let me go straight away. I couldn't see why we were treated like muck as we were British Rail Passengers and should be able to stay on the station. Trampas called us hooligans when we said we'd nearly been arrested and Sue and I were both close to tears. We went onto the platform with the Selby lot and some from Snaith and some Palace fans went past staring. I was past caring at this point. The following week as we got to the station we went to talk to Collar who we saw waiting there. One copper smiled at us and the others left us standing there, with the one who had been aggressive towards us last week not coming near us. After another match I walked from Elland Road with Mick from Selby and as we got to the station a copper was saying if you're not catching a train you couldn't go in. He saw me and said "hello ducks," I was surprised but he was a nice one. I suppose I was being recognised now and they knew I travelled in by train so was being allowed into the station.

It shows how attitudes were different in 1975 as Sue and I had some Leeds lads calling us names again when we were walking back to the station from Elland Road. When I asked a copper to tell them to stop it, he said there was nothing he could do.

On our way to Tottenham we were about an hour from Leeds and heard a bang and the Wallace Arnold coach swung from side to side. At first we thought a tyre had blown but think the bearings had gone. We kept going for a while and then stopped. The coppers came and escorted us off the motorway at the next turn off. We got off the coach and the lads went into a field full of clay hills and started throwing stones at each other. They went round with their trousers up to their knees and put bollards on their heads before the coppers came up and told them off. Because we were sat down the copper said he wasn't talking to us on the right but the stupid beings on the left of him. On the way back from the match we got pulled into the services by some more coppers because someone had thrown a can out of the window. They said they would keep us there until someone owned up, but then let us go after two minutes because no one did.

After a testimonial at Sunderland we left the ground at 10.00 pm and I followed Gary Edwards in my dad's car until he pulled his car in to the side of the road. We had followed him to see what they were up to, but realised they all wanted the loo so we carried on down the road. I pulled into the first services as the petrol gauge was on red and went straight for some petrol. I had to move round to the other side as the pump wouldn't reach, then had to put £1 notes in and filled up. Gary arrived shortly after us and as he filled up we saw the coppers arriving. The dog van arrived as we went into the services and then a black maria came and they went to check the pumps to see if we'd damaged them. I was raging and Tony was going to go and see them but didn't. One of the cop cars set off as we went to the car, probably to wait in a lay by but luckily didn't have any problems.

At the start of the 1976 season I saw a copper who knew me in Leeds station and he pointed and smiled. From there we went down to the Viaduct to see Gary Edwards and Gary Noble before carrying on to the Scarborough pub. The coppers weren't going to let some lads cross the road to it but we just walked in. At the station we had our friendly copper come up to us and say, 'Hello hooligans.' We started seeing him at every match on the station after this and he always spoke to us. Another copper with him said I'd changed my outfit and when I said I hadn't he said I was all white last season. Later as I was waiting for Carole to travel to an away match our friendly copper came out and said, "Since when have coaches gone from the station?" and I said I was waiting for Carole. He said if I missed the coach he would take me down in the car. When back in the station waiting for the train, I saw Ernie – from the Railway Police. He and his mate who knew me by sight wanted to know what I was doing in Leeds and I said I was on my way home.

Chapter Four – Coppers & Lads treatment of girls at football matches

Often at away matches Leeds fans were given a police escort to get us away from the ground as quick as possible. At Norwich there were 16 coaches in a line and it looked great but we had an over the top police escort which didn't leave us to our own devices until we were about 40 miles out of Norwich. Because of this we didn't stop until 2½ hours after we had left Norwich by which time I was in agony, as I needed the loo. The driver couldn't stop before because the coppers wouldn't let us, as they said Leeds fans steal too much.

When we arrived at Leicester and were getting off the coach a copper said, "This is mine" and I said, "I'm not" as all the lads got searched. As I was going into the ground a copper looked at me and I said, "You can't search me", he said "I can." I said, "You're not allowed" and he said, "We are" but they were laughing. I was right cheeky to them. The match was great and the Leeds fans chanted and sang and it was fantastic. They started scrapping with coppers though near the end of the match. They'll end up getting us banned if they don't watch it. At another match at Leicester in 1977 we queued up at the boys' entrance and the coppers were searching everyone. I said, "They're not touching me" and a lad said, "Well tell them you're a lass" and everyone laughed. The coppers were getting lads and throwing them out of the queue for the boys' entrance saying they weren't under 14 and got to Carole and I and the copper stood aside and let us in. We laughed our heads off inside and were telling everyone we'd got in.

At Elland Road, I was talking to Bob Vasey at the bus stop as about 50 Chelsea fans (a coach load) came down with three coppers following them. They looked right rough necks, skinheads, some black lads and some wearing donkey jackets. I followed them up to the Supporters Club and all the Chelsea fans tried getting into the yard at the front and the coppers threw them out and then went to tell the Leeds fans off who were outside the club. They blamed them for the Chelsea fans going in and said they were shouting at them over the wall. The fellas on the door came out and asked what was going on and the coppers told them and as they left I said the Leeds fans didn't do anything, it was the Chelsea fans who knew it was our club and came in to cause trouble. Eric Carlile came out and I told him what I'd seen and he said he believed me and was glad I was there to see what had happened.

Lads would always make comments to us and many of them were horrendous. We were called slags, sluts, scrubbers and whores just because we were girls and went to football matches. Lads thought they could touch us up all the time without a thought as to whether we wanted them to do it. The amount of times I had my bum nipped is unbelievable, which I suppose I should have taken as a compliment really. That is something I could cope with most of the time although if anyone tried I used to turn round and wack them one. We did get some nice things said too, but you tend to remember only the bad things. The one thing I definitely did not like is being touched up in a crowd, especially when lads tried to grope my boobs. The trouble was you couldn't always see who the culprit was so I just used to lash out at anybody and everybody. Once when Leeds were playing Newcastle at Elland Road, all the Geordie coaches were starting to arrive and loads were walking past the club as we came out to go into the ground. They were all oohing and aahing and then straight away one called us scrubbers. He got told where to go, as there was no need for any comments like that when they didn't even know us. It was a case of you were female and at a football match.

I was on the football special train coming back from Coventry and I'd had some lads chatting to me but all they seem to think about was sex, so I told them where to go. We had trouble at West Bromwich Albion for Johnny Giles testimonial; afterwards one Leeds lad asked us if they had raped us. When we said "No," he said, "They should have done." With fans like that you don't need enemies! We also had rude gestures made to us.

I saw Trampas and his friends who made some bad comments about us so I kicked one of them. I went on the football special again on my own to an away match at Derby in February 1975. I saw some lads I knew and although I was offered a place to sit I stayed standing. Some lads talked of gangbangs and made crude comments, as that's all they go on about but I just ignored them. When we arrived at Derby although we had an escort by the coppers, Leeds fans went on the rampage up Clifton Street smashing windows. I just followed the crowd up and down the street as everyone stayed together as that was the "safest" place for me to be. Also in the ground they tried to burn the stand down. It was a fantastic atmosphere at the match though. I ended up being hit by sheeting and a copper on a horse. On the way back on the special I sat with

Barry but found we were held up for three hours in Chesterfield. Apparently a lad was stabbed and the train wrecked but I am not sure of the details though. Two weeks later we played a rearranged match at Derby and I went on the football special, this time with Linda sitting with the Hull and Bridlington lot. We got very embarrassed because everything we said was turned the wrong way by the lads, so that the meaning was opposite to what we meant. This wasn't as bad as the name calling though because it was quite funny.

At Coventry we decided to go to the loos as soon as we got in the ground and thought we had gone the wrong way because we had to go down a passage then found both ladies and mens were next to each other. Not very good, because that meant the lads would more often than not use the ladies as well. We got into the ladies and some lasses went out and we heard the lads shouting and banging on the outer doors. We had just got into the loos when all the lads piled into the ladies and started banging on the cubicle doors. We didn't dare go out and I started shaking like a leaf. Pete Underwood came in and knew we were in there and started shouting at us and asking what we were doing so we said keeping you lot out. Eventually we decided to dive out of the loos as quickly as possible. Saw loads we knew who kept saying hello and some kept tapping me on the shoulder if I hadn't seen them. Saw the lad with curly hair from our coach to Belgium who said hello here's two troublemakers. One lad said he'd seen us last week. We got back to our places and we scored more or less immediately so we went mad and I accidentally knocked the Rangers fan in the eye with my elbow. At the end of the match we were all going down the road singing away. As we got to the coach park I heard a chant behind me of 'Heidi, Heidi show us your leg'; it was Vince and his mates and I could have died of embarrassment. Some lads on Dearneways coach shouted at me on the way out of the coach park. I had an argument with Billy because he nicked my hat and I dived to get it back but he kept thumping my arm, which hurt. One lad said I think you've gone too far Billy and he apologised later on.

On the way back from Tottenham on a Wallace Arnold coach, I started getting rude comments from some of the lads on the coach. One lad said something bad so I smacked him hard and told him not to say that to me again or he'd get more than he bargained for. At the services I saw Sue's coach pull in and went to find her and Mick, Alan and Paul. They said who's got a see through nightie and you look different with your clothes on. I dived into the loos and said to Sue that she had embarrassed me by showing them photos of us in Anderlecht and Barcelona. Sue said she had been embarrassed as well. One lad overheard me telling Carole and then started saying that I was always in bed and other bad things. I got very upset then because no matter what we said or didn't do the lads all thought we were having sex with every Tom, Dick and Harry. I just sat there and cried for half an hour and wouldn't speak to any of them. Karen came to talk to me about it and that set me off crying again. Some of the others started talking to me again and then Bob came and had an argument with me. Carole had got him to do that so that I would start talking again. Back at the station as I was getting my train ticket I heard someone say there's a Rangers fan and when I looked up I saw two man utd fans who asked why I supported rubbish. I said I didn't it was them who supported rubbish. They started going on about w***** Leeds so I said "Ipswich" to them and it shut them up as they had just been beaten by them. They then asked if I'd gone to Old Trafford and where I'd been. I said, "Yes, in the seats." They also said I wouldn't have worn my scarf outside would I? So I said, "no I didn't want my head kicking in" and then changed my mind and said, "Yes I did, it was wrapped around my waist."

Sue, Carole, Gary, Geoff, Alan, Paul and another lad met me in the station. We went to the little shop in the market and the woman asked me if I'd got married because there were so many lads with us so I said no, it's just our fan club. We went to Wallies and got our QPR tickets and then went up to the Gemini and met Jock and Collar on the way up. We decided to walk down to the ground and had about 30 lads following behind us.

In the ground Pete started being rude again saying I was a nympho, and going on about nipples and how big my boobs were. He upset me and I wouldn't speak to him and I said he could say what he liked to other people but not to bother saying them to me. I nearly started crying again. Sean said he didn't want anything to do with it. He said I had "nearly killed" a kid coming back from Celtic and had kicked hell out of him. The thing is if things were said once or twice I could take it as a joke, but instead it was every time I saw them and I had got sick to the back teeth of being seen as going to football matches looking for sex. For crying out loud why on earth would I spend all the money I had, nearly get my head kicked in every week just to look for lads to have sex with? Looking back at things now, I suppose it looked bad because I would talk to any of our fans. I was friends with a lot of them, there was a lot of banter and the lads enjoyed making me blush with embarrassment. But that still didn't make it acceptable for the way lads treated us for going to football matches, especially when we were such loyal supporters. I was quite naïve to a certain extent what with living in a village; it was completely different to living in a big city like Leeds. By lashing out at everyone I was trying to stick up for myself. At Leicester the following week I was stood with the normal gang and Pete Underwood was there. He asked if I'd forgiven him and I said no. He said "Please forgive me I'll kiss your feet" so I said, "Get down on the floor then" and he did, so I forgave him.

On the way back from a match Neil kept coming round me and touching my leg and I told him to keep his hands to himself. The rest of the lads were coming out with filthy comments. We had stopped at Watford Gap but we weren't allowed in so carried on to Leicester Forest on the M1 and found coppers everywhere. Sheffield Wednesday and Leeds fans had been causing trouble and ours had smashed one of their coaches up. As we got off the coach Alan kicked one of theirs going past and the coppers got him and arrested him and threw him in the back of their van. I think he'll get sent down as he's got a bad record and he's got to go to court over a Chesterfield incident two weeks ago. I got attacked by some of the lads on the coach and they stretched me by my scarves and were all trying to grab me. They were too rough and I don't know what I did to deserve it. They put a hole in my scarf as well which I wasn't happy about. Neil wants to go to the Scotland/England match with me but no chance, as I knew what he wanted and he won't get it. Carole told me later that when her and Sue walked back to the station she saw Neil and he was with a gang of rough looking lads who she hadn't seen before and he asked where I was. She said I wasn't with them and I didn't like him and this other lad said "is that her who you shagged last week?" So Carole said he never laid a finger on her and he won't. The next time I saw Neil he said, "I hear you're not friends with me." I said, "Do you blame me?" and he said "it wasn't me it was the others." As he started talking to me I saw him in a different light, which showed he wasn't so bad after all.

In the Kop I stood in front of Collar and at half-time he grabbed me so I hit him and he said, "Give over you love it." I got upset about some rude comments from Brod and some of the others. I was walking out with Tich and Frank when Tich told me to ignore what was said to me and I just said, "I wished people would leave me alone." I said to Carole I wasn't coming anymore. We all left at 5.35 pm and I said I'd see everyone on Wednesday and Mac said he thought I wasn't coming anymore and I said, "Oh dear I'd forgotten, I always did have a short memory." I enjoyed the match though but not the teasing and as I went back to the car I could have sat there and cried. I know some of the teasing is light hearted but it gets very wearing.

Chapter Five

Doncaster, a football special and Hillsborough

15 August 1973 is a day that I will never forget, an evening friendly at Belle Vue, the home of Doncaster Rovers. I went by car from Carlton with Dave, Timmy, Sue and Liz. This was the first football match that Liz had been to. This also ended up as the first match where I was on the receiving end of violence. The only entrances were at one end of the ground and when we got in we decided to walk all the way round to be behind the goal at the far side and stood right at the front. The main Doncaster fans were located down the side, as we were in early there were no problems, but things were about to change. The match hadn't even kicked off when a group of eight girls came up behind us. One of them came up to Liz and threatened her and because she had never been to a match before I told them to leave her alone. That was when all eight attacked me, I fended off the blows as best as I could and then I found myself at the other side of the wall on the side of the pitch. They then asked Sue if she was with me and she said she wasn't and the lads I was with 'disowned' me as well. The ringleader of the girls shouted, "Come on" to me as she wanted to take me on, on her own. My retort was, "Yes you and all your mates". I stayed where I was and luck was on my side when the lad who had been stood at the side of me (Graham) told them to get lost. He seemed to know them and after a few arguments they indeed went away. I think I was targeted because I 'looked' hard, wearing my white dungarees, had short hair and I was wearing the monkey boots that Janet had given me. The fact was though that it couldn't have been further from the truth. As I climbed back over the wall, the lad told me that he was a Liverpool supporter and he had pushed me over the wall to get me out of the way. I couldn't remember how I ended up over the wall but

was grateful for the help. Sue and the lads apologised for not helping me but obviously didn't want to end up getting attacked as well.

Because of this I became very anxious as the match progressed, especially as there were fights breaking out along the front of the side where the Doncaster fans were. Every time Leeds lads were spotted there was scrapping. As you had to go past there to get outside the ground I became very worried. After discussions between us all we decided we would leave the match early and go back to the car. To do this we ended up going across the rear of the stand up a steep banking to avoid the stand and the trouble. The Liverpool fan came with us and once again I was grateful for his help. Unfortunately the football had faded into the background and I had been introduced first hand to football violence. We actually won the match 2–0 with goals from Jones and Cherry. I got home to my sisters and then burst into tears through the shock. I went to work the next day where I worked on reception, but found I couldn't wear the headphones due to pain around my ears which was probably because of bruising I had sustained in the attack.

I had been quite blasé up till then regarding violence as I had always managed to hide my colours and avoid it. This had an effect on me that would last forever as I would shake with fear many times over the coming years. It also made me more observant of what was happening around me at or going to and from football matches, although it didn't stop me wearing my colours. This though was probably why trouble started to follow me around.

The next match on 18 August 1973 saw us go to Huddersfield for the semi-final of the West Riding Cup. Sue and I decided to go on the football special train to this one. Coming back the journey took 2¼ hours to travel the short distance from Huddersfield to Leeds. Sue and I got on the train to go back and as there were no seats we had to stand. The carriage we were in had separate compartments and we went into one of them, which was full of Leeds fans. The train hadn't been going long, before lads were coming down the corridors and going to the front carriage, which was a seated carriage with tables in between the seats if I remember correctly. A lad saw us in the compartment and came in and told Sue and I that under no circumstances were we to leave the carriage as it wasn't safe. This time was one of great fear for us both as we thought we would get attacked by our own fans. The lads who had gone to the front carriage proceeded to smash it to bits. When we eventually arrived at Leeds we had to go out through the door leading into the first carriage. It was a shock to see there was nothing left of the carriage only lots of wooden splinters. A posse of coppers met us and unfortunately because we had been on the train, this led to Sue and I being treated as guilty by association. The coppers wouldn't let us go and get our train for Selby and were made to leave the station. We ended up having to eventually go back in the main entrance to get back onto the platform to catch our train home. I don't know if they ever charged anybody for the damage but it was definitely a journey you would never forget.

Saturday 23 April 1977 saw the FA Cup semi-final against man utd at Hillsborough. Carole met me in Leeds and we went into town passing the lads off the Wallies coach and they said, "It's the Queen of the coach." When we arrived in Sheffield I decided to leave my banner on the coach, as I didn't want it to get pinched. The Lancashire Whites coach from Bolton was in front of ours. When we got off the coach one lad from Bolton said *Daily Express*, he always shouts it at us and asked why we hadn't mentioned him – Andy from Bolton? I went and got my programmes and a man utd fan shouted hey Billy Bremner at me. I left the programmes on the coach, met Linda and Steve and we all went down to the ground together and saw there were man utd fans all over the place. I was sure something was going to happen as not many coppers were about but we got to the ground okay.

When we got to the turnstiles where the Leeds fans were to go in, we had a shock to find that loads of man utd fans were in our end and queuing to get in. As soon as I got inside a man utd fan called me a prostitute and I said, "I am not" and he said "You are" so I thought p*** off. When I got in the ground I stood talking to a lass from Doncaster who was on the Advance coach and saw that even more man utd fans were coming in. It ended up with the standing area being split in two with Leeds fans nearer the entrances into the ground and the man utd fans at the other side with a walkway in between both sets of fans. There were approx 2,000 man utd at the other side of the stand when six Leeds lads stood at the back of our side started chanting and singing. I went to the loo and had to go through their side and make my way through the reds, which wasn't very nice. I met up with Linda and Steve again in our side and we made our way into the stand and stood halfway down the terracing with a barrier in front of us. More Leeds fans were arriving and some were coming in side by side with the man utd fans and started braying them. Leeds fans started singing and shut their fans up. It got quite packed where we were and everyone was falling against the barrier so Linda, Steve and I moved in front of it and I ended up with a bruise on my back from the crush. The match started and after 15 minutes we were two goals down and our dream of going to Wembley again had ended.

The barrier behind us had bent almost double with the pressure of the fans so we moved down and got against another barrier and then everyone piled down with Linda and I crushed against it. I was nearly bent double; I'd got it in my side and Linda in her ribs. We were screaming and crying and eventually our lads got us out and underneath the barrier to safety. I couldn't stop crying and I thought I'd bust my thumb. I was shaking like a leaf and Linda nearly fainted. A lad put his arms round us both and comforted us and they were all really great with us. I saw June and she asked what the matter was and we moved down and got a copper to get us to the front of the terracing. Saw a load we knew and they were all asking what was wrong, as I was still crying. We got out onto the pitch side and had to walk past all the man utd fans to the corner where the first aid was and they were all shouting at us. As we stood by the corner flag I heard someone shout Heidi and saw it was a man utd fan I knew from Selby. We stayed in the first aid until 3.50 pm. Pete Underwood was in there too so I sat next to him along with some man utd fans and one wanted to rub me better. As we were going back into the ground the lad from Selby asked if I still loved him and I said I'd tell him next week. We got called prostitutes again from some man utd fans and saw some getting carried out covered in blood.

Carole shouted us and a steward from Leeds asked what had happened so we told them. I stood for the second half with Carole, Margaret and some others. Richard lent me his parker because I was cold (suffering from shock). Just before the end of the match we moved to the side but they'd locked us in and everyone was getting crushed and going onto the pitch. I managed to get out and back to Carole and we went out of the back entrance and all the Leeds fans were singing we hate man u and they scattered and chased them.

There were a few coppers around and we got back to the coach park. We heard afterwards that Leeds got loads of man utd fans especially at half-time, and only a few Leeds got done. Went straight to the Gemini when we got back to Leeds and found loads of Leeds fans in singing who all thought I'd got beaten up. Everyone was talking about man utd fans getting "killed" at half-time. Went to the Three Legs and again everyone was singing and standing on seats and you wouldn't have thought we'd lost. I was literally falling all over the place when I went for the train and then I was sick and not very well as usual. Dad and Arthur picked me up in Selby. Next day I was aching all over and showed my mum all my bruises.

Later one of Kevin and Bob's friends Pete said I'd got beaten up at Hillsborough and I said, "No I got crushed by a barrier." He said, "I thought you'd got beaten up so I went mad and said look, them two lasses have got done and I'm going to 'kill' man utd" and a copper said, "Go ahead" then kicked him out. There were all man utd fans there so he came back in again. He was going to 'kill' them because he thought they'd done us in.

Chapter Six

Trouble follows me around

Leeds United won the league in 1969 and I was there for the last home match of the season when we played Nottingham Forest. The match and atmosphere had been superb and it had been a great night. I also found out the hard way that you should never wear your scarf loosely around your neck. After the match we had gone for an ice cream before going back to the coach and then the unbelievable happened to me, someone pinched my scarf! I was heartbroken and cried all the way home because something like that had happened.

The 1972–1973 season also saw more trouble starting to appear at the matches. On 9 September 1972, I can always remember the day my nephew Mark was born. Leeds were playing at Stoke and I went on the football special with some of the lads from where I lived. I didn't see any trouble before or during, but after the match was different. I can remember all the Leeds fans on the special were getting in a group at the back of the stand near the end of the match. Someone said that we should all stick together going back to the station. I'm not sure if I had hidden my scarf at this point or shortly after, but we were running down the street back to the station when we were 'ambushed' at the graveyard. Stoke fans had been hiding there and when we got near it they started throwing things and then all ran out at the Leeds fans. I was stood on the street corner and everyone had scattered, Stoke fans were grabbing hold of lads and saying, "Who are you, Leeds or Stoke?" When they said Stoke they were let go. I think because I was female no one spoke to me or threatened me. When I realised I was safe I carried on walking towards the station and all of a sudden a couple of the lads I had travelled with appeared by my side. There were Stoke fans with 'make up' all over their faces, basically copying the thugs in 'A Clockwork Orange', who were lined up along the street going to the station. Luckily we made it back there in one piece and when we got on our train saw there was a train on the opposite platform full of Stoke fans but nothing else happened. I got back home to find out that my sister Karin had given birth to Mark so the day had a happy ending!

The next match that caused problems was Aston Villa away in the Football League Cup third-round held on 11 October 1972 where I spent the grand sum of 90p all in. I went on a Wallace Arnold coach and we got to the ground just as the match kicked off and didn't see any trouble there. The match ended up as a 1–1 draw with our goal being scored by Jack Charlton. I was getting used to hiding my scarf going back to the coaches and there were a group of Villa fans stood on the corner of the street that we had to walk through. Apart from asking some of the lads "what time is it mate?" where they didn't get an answer, they didn't bother us. Asking the time was a trick to find out what accent the lads spoke with. Obviously if they spoke with a Yorkshire accent then they must be Leeds fans! We got back on the coach and I am sure that the Wallace Arnold coach we were on was the only one that went to the match and wasn't totally full. We were about five minutes away from the ground stuck in traffic when the bricks started flying at the coach. A lad told me to get down on the floor in the middle of the coach as we were being hit from all different angles. It took eight bricks before the window next to me went through. It was absolutely terrifying and I was scared stiff. Eventually after they had put two large windows through and cracked a third everything went quiet and we were left to survey the damage, luckily we were all okay. It was absolutely freezing on the coach going home to Leeds and to make it worse we hit freezing fog on the motorway. Unfortunately events took another turn for the worse when a half-caste lad on the coach decided he was going to throw the seats out of the broken window onto the motorway. He proceeded to throw two out of the window and I was so scared at this time that I moved to the front of the coach. If someone hit those there surely would be a nasty accident!

At Aston Villa again in 1977 we had trouble again. We left the coach park and Carole and I went round by the Church and bought a badge then we took our scarves off. All the rest of the Leeds fans went down the road we'd just travelled down on the coach. We'd got to the Holte End pub and spotted the

Leeds lot coming down the side road and all the Villa fans ran up in front of them. We got so far down the road and all the Leeds fans came charging past us with Villa after them and the Leeds lot shouting stop, don't run, fight. Karen got chased down an alley by five lads and then they said it's a bird and left her. The coppers stopped them all and we walked past them to the ground. At the beginning of the second half a few Villa ended up behind us and the Leeds lot kept moving away. We stayed there until just before the end when we moved near the entrance. At the end we walked out with no scarves on and stayed behind some Villa fans. All the Villa fans were coming out of the Holte End and coming down to the Witton End where we were. As we passed the Holte End someone said, "where's your scarves?" and someone shouted "There's Heidi there." We got down to the coaches okay after we'd come through a gang of kids. A kid came up to me in the coach park and said can you tell me the time please my watch is bust. I thought it's the oldest trick in the book but seeing as we were at the coaches and a copper was there I told him 10 to five. The majority of Leeds fans got back okay.

We left the coach park and were just going up by Spaghetti Junction when we got bricked and a window smashed. The driver stopped the coach and all the lads dived off the coach and chased them. I've never seen anyone run so fast. A fella who witnessed the attack said, "go and get the b******s lads." They chased a service bus because a Villa fan was going to get off but he decided against it and the bus carried on. The lads came back to the coach, as the coppers arrived and came on to our coach and hit any lad standing up saying what's going on? They were horrible but it wouldn't have happened if they'd escorted us away from the ground. The coppers went and left us and we carried on and we got bricked again and it came through Ian's side of the window, straight across the coach and smashed our window. It had hit Ian's head and just missed Carole's and mine. The driver didn't stop this time and we smashed the windows out and then got bricked again with no window and we just ducked, I was waiting for the brick to hit me but luckily it didn't, it hit lower down the side of the coach. I put my hand down and said thank goodness and put my finger straight on some glass and cut it deep and it wouldn't stop bleeding.

We got stopped further up the road by some more coppers for throwing glass out of the window. They said they'd had reports that bottles and cans had been thrown out too when they are not even allowed on the coaches. They said if it happened again we'd all be in the nick for the night. I was so angry by this time that I went down to the front of the coach to complain to the coppers that we were the victims and I had been injured by the coach getting bricked. I said the windows had been smashed and we were covered in glass. They then said they would get another coach to meet us at Trowell Services. It was cold until Trowell and we were all shouting, singing and waving to everyone when going through Derby. We got to the services at 7.30 pm and had to wait until 8.45 pm for another coach because the coppers hadn't given Wallies the message to send another coach for us. Got to Leeds eventually at 10.40 pm and the driver dropped Carole and I off at the station. I rang mum up to say I may have to go to hospital yet then caught the 10.55 pm train and sat next to Les Smith and a lad from Burn. That horrible scouser was on and he called me a b*****d so I told him to get lost. My finger eventually stopped bleeding but was swollen so I decided I didn't need to go to hospital but would bathe it instead.

We arrived at Derby for an FA Cup tie at the Baseball Ground and because we needed the loo Helen, Christine and I walked past the ground and found a pub. On our way back to join the Leeds fans we literally bumped into a gang of approx 50 Derby fans that swarmed across the whole road. Christine got hit, they tried to nick my banner and we got spat and sworn at. Luckily we managed to get through them relatively in one piece but it was pretty scary. At Coventry with atrocious weather conditions of freezing driving rain and sleet, I found this was a very unnerving night at a football match because I felt you couldn't trust opposing fans. There was only one Wallace Arnold coach there as far as I am aware and some Coventry fans made a beeline for us in the ground. They came and stood next to us and then started counting our scarves and some asked me where I was from. Although they didn't do anything to us, when we moved away they followed us, which made me very edgy.

27 September 1975 and Burnley away, we went on the service train from Leeds to Todmorden and then a service bus from there direct to the ground. We then went to a pub where they only let non-hooligans in and as we obviously didn't look like hooligans, they let us in. When we came out we went to see if the coaches had arrived but they hadn't. On our way back to the pub these kids were outside the souvenir shop and as they came across the road to

us I saw they were Burnley fans. Some Leeds fans came round the corner just as we crossed the road and a banger exploded at my feet. We shouted at the Leeds fans to get them so they ran after them. One lad commented, "Did you see that, those lasses told the lads to chase them and they did!"

Met Dillon and Steve who tagged along with us and eventually we went in a pub packed full of Leeds fans singing away and it was great. We saw the Burnley fans going past the pub with an escort. We then went to the ground and were surprised to see some Leeds fans with blood pouring from their heads from being bricked. The twins had also been hit. Dillon ended up with appendicitis at half-time. Scunny kept saying that he had seen us crying in Paris and loads kept saying it's the *Daily Express* girls. After the match we went down to see the players off. I said to Billy "well played" and he looked up and said, "Thank you love" and Peter said hello to us. As we were talking to the driver of the team coach a Burnley fan walked past and spat in Karen's face. Linda shouted at him and he said come on you f****** Leeds c**** so Linda went and belted him one. He was about 25 and dressed in a raincoat and no scarf. I hope he was proud of himself the coward, as he waited until the majority of Leeds fans had gone and picked on some girls, but he soon disappeared after Linda had hit him. We then got the bus back to Todmorden and on reaching the bus stop we saw some Burnley fans waiting. As we got off the bus some coppers came round the corner in a car so Carole asked for an escort. We got back just in time to catch the train having run most of the way. Tony decided to run across the railway lines and got done by the coppers for it.

Another away match where trouble followed me was the visit to Ipswich on 13 December 1975. We lost the match 2–1 with McKenzie scoring our goal. I went on the Advance coach from Goole. Billy and his dad came to pick me up from Carlton at 6.00 am then got taken to Goole to pick the coach up where some lads from Old Goole got on as well. Jonathan and Nicholas were picked up at Rawcliffe and more lads along the way including Joe and Goof from Thirsk. Billy's mum and Bev his sister got on as well although I didn't realise they were all one family until then. At Doncaster Ian Lattimore and Malcolm Day got on. They started eating and drinking straight away and I didn't know how they could, as I couldn't face anything. I was absolutely frozen as there was no heating on the coach and was glad to stop at the services. The

Pontefract coach stopped as well and as we were going into the services they started banging on the windows and singing they all loved t**s. It was well embarrassing and as I was going to the loo someone nipped my bum. We arrived at Ipswich at 11.15 am and got to the ground at 11.45 am. We had seen the Pontefract lot running down the road when we got there.

We went straight to the pub when we got there as we were cold and just as we were going up to the Sporting Farmer about 30 to 40 Ipswich fans were coming up the road and started shouting and running after us. There were about 15 of us. Got into the pub and the lads went to sit down whilst I went to the loo because as usual I was shaking like a leaf. When I came out the Ipswich fans were standing round whilst our lot were sat in the corner near the bar so I went to join them. I heard some Ipswich fans saying there's a bird with them. I got a pineapple juice and the lads said let Heidi sit down so I sat at the back between Wish and a skinhead. I couldn't stop shaking and the lads were saying don't worry and ignore them. The Ipswich fans were eyeing us up and piling bottles and glasses onto the table in the middle. They heard the Pontefract lads go past but didn't go after them. Eventually they went out of the pub and I gave a sigh of relief but I was still worried and couldn't drink anything else or I would have been sick. Ian said I would be a nervous wreck before I was 17. Some of the Supporters Club lot came in and I felt a bit safer seeing more Leeds fans in the pub. After a while the doors of the pub swung open and about 80 to 100 Ipswich fans came in singing an IRA song. I thought we'd had it because this was an aggro song. We couldn't get out of the pub as our path to the door was blocked. They started singing we all f***** hate Leeds and if one of our fans would have said anything we'd have had it as all the bottles and glasses were still piled up on the table in front of them. Some of the Supporters Club lot left and Pete Spence got booted on his way out. I shoved my two scarves up my jacket as I didn't want them nicked and also put my camera there as well. One lad saw me and kept smirking. Next minute the landlord of the pub told them all to get out or he'd call the cops and they went. I could have collapsed and if I hadn't have been sat down I'd have been in a heap on the floor.

A bit later the door opened again and 20 Leeds hards walked in with Alan from Seacroft. He wanted to know why I'd been scared. One lad said to

Ian that they nearly had a fit when they saw us sat there as calm as anything because the Sporting Farmer is where the Ipswich hards hang out. Finally we left the pub at approx 2.15 pm so I had been literally shaking for 2½ hours. Saw Jock in the ground so paid him the coach fare for the trip to Rangers. The lads off our coach came up to me and asked if I'd be okay after the match and I said yes thanks. I took a picture of Bob Vasey and Kevin Sharp (he went on to play cricket for Yorkshire) and they called me a traitor for not going on their coach. I got a picture of Leeds fans singing *'You'll never walk alone'* too. When Ipswich scored Leeds fans went mad and started fighting with the coppers. Luckily we were hemmed in by the barriers and managed to keep out of the trouble. Ipswich fans had nicked our songs and after the match they had all disappeared. Met the Wallies lot who asked why I wasn't on the number one coach and that I should have booked on it. Carole said they were all singing 'who took the North Bank Highbury, Heidi'. On the way back talked to Mark, Billy, Bev and Ian most of the way. Billy was 19 and Bev and Mark were trying to guess how old I was, 17 or 18. I wouldn't tell them at first but then confessed I was 20 and they thought I was younger than Billy. Got back to Rawcliffe at 9.15 pm and Jonathan's mum and dad gave me a lift home. Watched Leeds on *Match of the Day* and kept nearly passing out.

The following week I went to the Peacock pub at Elland Road and Alan J. asked why I'd been scared at Ipswich? I told him that I'm afraid that's the way I am, probably getting beaten up at Doncaster Rovers made things worse, because before that it wasn't a problem and also I feel that lots of the lads are tougher than I am.

Wednesday 1 March 1978 we travelled to Old Trafford to play man utd. Leeds won the match 1–0 with a goal from Clarke. Aunty Annie and Angela (man utd fans) came through to Cowick Hall where I worked and we set off at 5.00 pm but stopped off at Elland Road to pick the others up. In Mick's car were Ian, Bob and Martin and in Dad's car Aunty Annie, Angela, Carole, Sharon and myself. As we got to the Yorkshire services we said we'd stop for toilets. We got back to the car but there was no sign of the lads so I said I'd go back and get them. I shouted them to hurry up and found out they'd gone for a cup of tea. Was going back to the car with Mick and heard the others coming behind us so I turned round and Bob came running towards me and said give me your body or something to that effect and I put my hands up to keep him away and he stuck a knife straight in my thumb. It was an accident, as I didn't know he'd got a knife and he was only messing about but it backfired big style. My thumb was bleeding like mad and I still had to drive to Manchester with my thumb throbbing like mad and the hankies covered in blood.

We got stuck in traffic nearing the ground and when we got to the Trafford Park Hotel I noticed a space so we pulled in and Mick did the same at the side of us. We blocked someone in but we weren't bothered because it was 7.10 pm. Got to the ground and there was no chance of us getting in the scoreboard seats so Aunty Annie said to go in the Stretford End instead. We got round there and seats were still available so we got in there for £1 each. We didn't mouth it because there were loads of roughnecks about and they could easily have got in the seats from the Stretford standing below us. We got sat down and the teams came out and I said I'd have a look at my thumb and nearly died because it was all swollen up and bleeding. I decided that I'd go to the first aid and Sharon said she'd come with me. So we went and a steward took us round underneath the stand by the Stretford paddock and terracing into the first aid. I spotted Dale coming up the tunnel limping, he'd done his ankle in and he asked what I'd done and I said I'd fallen. We told them in the first aid that we were Leeds fans then got back to the seats ten minutes after kick off. A man utd fella sat behind us in the seats had asked Carole what had happened and had I been stabbed and she said yes. He said I bet it was a Leeds fan because man utd fans wouldn't do that so she said well yes it was.

When Clarkie scored the ball slowly trickled across the goal line right in front of the Stretford End and right in front of where we were sat. We stood up with everyone else and had to pretend we weren't Leeds fans, but were absolutely ecstatic and trying hard not to laugh and cheer. At the end of the match after we'd won – Super Team, stayed in the stand to go to the toilets and then go to the souvenir shop to meet Angela and Bob (her boyfriend who we were giving a lift back.). There were loads of man utd fans waiting outside the scoreboard because they'd kept the Leeds fans in. We got back to the car and had passed Phil from Scarborough and spoke. When we reached the car I saw four lads stood around it and nearly had a fit because I thought they'd seen the Leeds GB sticker (I'd covered it in mud). The lads said hooray they're here because we'd blocked them in. I apologised and one lad said he'd watch so I could pull out onto the road and pull back onto the side because we had to wait for Mick. The lads were right nice and waved when they went but it might have been a different matter if they'd have known we were Leeds fans. We had to wait ages for Ian and Mick to come. Whilst we were waiting about 15 man utd fans came past with bricks looking for the Leeds coaches and a couple looked at us all but carried on. I felt it was a good job we had Aunty Annie, Angela and Bob with us. Just after that at approx 10.00 pm Ian and Mick arrived, they'd been jumped on by about 50 man utd fans as they came out of the escort and a black lad had started it, with Ian coming off worst. We got in both cars; we'd got Bob as an extra now, and went to see my friend Liz for a cup of tea who lived nearby then set off back at 11.15 pm.

At a match at Nottingham Forest we tried getting in their Supporters Club but were not allowed in; on our way back to the car park a copper said it wasn't safe for us to be walking around like that. We stood by the coaches and five minutes later some Forest fans came looking for bother and they smashed the team coach and another coach up. Luckily they opened the gates then to let us in and there were loads of Leeds fans there. To go to the loo we had to go into the Forest side and got some funny looks from these Forest lads as we were wearing our colours. At the end of the match we went out and the Forest fans were all amongst the cars in the car park and we had to get through them to go to the coaches. We got called some names, were followed by some Forest fans and by the time we got to the coach I was shaking like a leaf.

Chapter Seven

Leeds fans, The Gelderd End/Kop
& Wallace Arnold coaches

When I first started following Leeds away from home to the matches that were far away, I had to travel from Leeds as both York Pullman and Abbey Coachways didn't run to these matches. As I booked my tickets at the Corn Exchange prior to the match I always ended up on Wallace Arnold number one coach (Wallies Trollies). You could turn up on the morning of the match and buy your ticket but I liked to know that I had got mine. For some matches there were only one or two Wallace Arnold coaches that went so this meant that I got to know the regulars on the coach over the years and many are all still good friends to this day. This also meant that I became part of a group of Leeds fans following Leeds everywhere including my friends Sue and Carole. Others at that time were Margaret, Gary Edwards, Gary Noble, Christine, Collar, Colleen, Esther, Ray and Maureen to name a few. You also got to know the regular coach drivers on Wallace Arnold coaches. When Leeds played Cardiff in an FA Cup match I slept a lot of the way there. When we were driving over the Severn Bridge I commented on the fact that I hated going over the water and it made me very anxious as I had a fear of water. Well all that did was make the driver drive over the bridge at a crawl whilst he was laughing at me! We had an excellent relationship with the regular drivers though and they always looked after us. For example, when Len drove us to Tottenham he took us straight to the ground instead of dropping us off at King's Cross.

Carole and Margaret were always on our coach and I stood next to them at a night match at Birmingham as we arrived just after kick-off. We all stood behind the goal and I saw them throwing chewing gum to Gary Sprake which apparently they did at every away match.

On 1 November 1975 came a trip to Derby and a 3–2 defeat. At the services there were loads of Leeds coaches in. We weren't allowed to get to Derby until 2.00 pm at the earliest (as instructed by the coppers) and didn't leave the services until 2.10 pm. Eight Wallace Arnold coaches arrived together and when they were all going down the road, it looked great. When we got to the Derby car park at 2.30 pm they were only letting one coach in at a time and searching all the lads as they got off the coach. We had to run all the way to the ground and I was shattered by the time we got there. Got in the ground and whilst waiting for Sue and Carole saw the Halifax lads who called me a hooligan. There were loads of Leeds fans in the ground down the Popular side. When Norman got sent off for smacking Francis Lee it was the first time I really felt like 'kicking someone.' As we were moving towards the entrance near the end of the match Derby scored and I banged this fan on his back once in a temper although this was something that I wasn't proud of when I looked back at my behaviour. Leeds fans started scrapping and Derby fans had to run onto the pitch to get away. When we got out of the ground we had to go down the narrow ginnel to get to the coaches and saw that some Leeds fans had smashed some windows along the way prior to the ginnel. Carole came back onto the coach and was swearing like mad about Norman getting sent off and said she had jumped on the fence and a copper told her if she didn't get off she would be arrested. The Popular terrace was low down at the front with a fence across the wall and she had jumped up against it. Up to that point we had never heard Carole swear or even say bloody before so Sue and I collapsed in hysterics because it sounded so funny. The following week I saw Violet who said that a hooligan lad they didn't know had asked where I was and said that everywhere he went he saw me. He had been near me at Derby and had also seen us in the paper.

Southampton away on 15 September 1973 was always destined to turn out the way it did. First of all my brother-in-law Terry who was working in Leeds set off without picking me up. Although he must have come back for me, because I ended up catching a Wallace Arnold coach which then broke down at Oxford. Somehow we ended up on a relief coach and unfortunately this also broke down 25 miles from Southampton. After that I think Phil Beeton managed to hire a further coach for £15 and we all shared the cost of this. Christine and Helen thumbed a lift from the services and managed to get there in time for kick off but I was too scared to do this. We eventually arrived at the ground at 4.30 pm and some fans were already leaving the match. Clarke had scored twice in a 2–1 win and if I remember rightly I think we saw the Saints goal, although my memory might be playing tricks. We then went to a pub near the ground as we had to wait until 7.30 pm before a relief coach came to take us back to Leeds. We sang all the way back from the match and everyone joined in.

In December 1975 we got on Wallace Arnold coach number one to go to Arsenal. All our lads had got on coach two by mistake but as soon as they saw us, they all came and got onto our coach. We had a little singsong going down but not much and when we stopped at the services I took some photos of our lads. Halfway home after the match I went round for a collection for the driver and had to 'wake' half of the lads up as they were pretending to be asleep. As I was returning to the back of the coach I was attacked by the front seat boys' and tied to a seat by my scarves. Sue and Karen came to help me and the same happened to them. We had a right 'fight' with them all. We managed to get back to our seats and then the front seat boys tried to take the back seat but they didn't succeed. All the lads at the back helped us and took a hostage. We were all singing away and the back seat stretched to where the front seat boys were. I took plenty of photos of this day.

The following January saw us visit Wolverhampton. The top window on the coach was open so I shut it because we were cold and the lads kept opening it. In the end the driver came and shut it and as I was stood up the lads started hitting my bum. It hurt so I screamed and all the ones sat at the front of the coach looked round and laughed. I moved towards the front of the coach and then turned round to hit some back and Ian started to take photos of me. I went to hit Bob for hitting me and I punched him in the face accidentally and bent his finger back. I think I dislocated it and I couldn't stop apologising because I didn't actually mean to do it. I didn't dare to do the collection for the driver in case they attacked me again so Ian did it.

Whenever we girls fell out, it was normally when we had been drinking. Karen got very upset because I got on well with the lads and she thought I would go after her boyfriend. I would never do that, but she said I played lads up and got them worked up. I didn't look at it like that as I was just friends with them and all the others got boyfriends and were asked out, not me. Because of this Karen said that she should go to away matches on her own as she felt 'I was a threat to her and any relationship she wanted'. We all went out one evening and got quite drunk then Karen got upset and started saying it's all Heidi and she's sick of it being Heidi all the time. I said to Carole what could I do because everything I do is wrong. The reason she is like that is because of me, it's all my fault. She hates everyone saying my name and I started to cry. The next morning I couldn't see straight and the room was going round and round. Later when we walked up to Karens I got a right lecture about me always being the centre of attention. It's always Heidi this and that and it's Heidi's gang. I was so sick of it all that I said, "it's not worth saying anything because I'd be wrong". Karen said that she was right and no one can prove her wrong. As usual though, we made friends again very quickly and all was forgotten.

For the Chelsea away match on 15 December 1973 a number of us hired our own coach and were staying in London until midnight. There were a lot of Leeds fans there and we won the match 2–1 with Jordan and Jones scoring our goals. I'm not sure if we chanted Leeds or cheered when we scored but all of a sudden Chelsea fans charged at us all. We were behind the goal to the left of the stand. It was a quick, hide your scarf, situation but luckily by doing this quickly we managed to stay incognito. At the end of the match we got a tube back to King's Cross where the coach was parked. We then found a pub nearby and stayed there until closing. There were Sunderland fans in the vicinity too but in the pub it was just Leeds fans. This was a time for celebrations with Sue and me paralytic by the end of the night. We each had ten bacardi and cokes and were crawling around the toilets on our hands and knees, singing Leeds songs at the tops of our voices. It is also something I have never forgotten, as I have never touched bacardi again from that day to this.

Sue and I travelled to Manchester on Friday evening with Arthur prior to the match against man utd on 9 February 1974. Arthur lived with his family in Urmston next door to Brian Greenhoff, which wasn't far from Old Trafford and we were going to stay the night there. We caught a service bus to the ground the next morning and nearly got thrown off because we were Leeds fans. We got to the ground early and bought tickets for the seats in the scoreboard end. We also heard that a Leeds lass had been attacked (kicked) by approx 20 man utd lads. After the match we walked back to Urmston and we felt that we stood out like a sore thumb as only Sue and I didn't have any colours on. It was a very uncomfortable feeling because we felt sure that everyone knew we were Leeds fans although we managed to get back to Urmston in one piece. It was also a fantastic day because Leeds won the match 2–0 with Jones and Jordan scoring our goals. It was also the highest attendance approx 57,000 if I remember correctly.

The FA Cup replay against Bristol City took place in February 1974 and we ended up getting beaten 1–0. It was almost unheard of for Leeds to lose, especially at home. I was that upset that I sat down in the Kop and started crying only to have a lad tell me off. He said I shouldn't be so daft. Losing was something that we had to get used to over time. In these early days of supporting Leeds we got so used to winning matches and if we got a draw at home that used to be a catastrophe, because we had dropped a point (it was two points for a win at this time).

31 March 1975, at the end of a busy month of football matches, saw the visit of Leicester City to Elland Road. The match was a 2–2 draw with Clarke and Giles scoring for Leeds. This is the only match that I went to totally paralytic along with Sue, having downed ten gin and bitter lemons in the Supporters Club before the match. Carole had taken her sister Ruth to the match and she had introduced us to her. Ruth's comments were that we were a bit inebriated weren't we! I can remember leaving the club but can't remember getting into the ground. I can remember singing in the toilets in the Kop at the top of my voice but somehow I ended up losing my purse with my train ticket home. I'm afraid I didn't see much of the match in my drunken stupor but did wake up in time to see Leeds score two goals to make it a draw. Someone said I had been sick in someone's crash helmet but I hadn't. It can't have been a big crowd either as we sat on the terraces at the top of the Kop. It was also the drink that made me feel very sorry for myself and I ended up being very dramatic with suicidal thoughts. Luckily Jonathan and Nicholas, friends of ours from Rawcliffe lent me the money to get home. I

never touched gin and bitter lemon again or drank that much before a match either.

For the FA Cup sixth round in March 1975 at Ipswich Town I went on the special train taking my banner with me. On arrival some Ipswich fans commented that we were Gelderd Boot girls. Loads of Leeds fans came to meet the special when it arrived at Ipswich and I thought it was great to see so many of our fans there. The replay at Elland Road with Ipswich came the following week and I got a lift in from work with a colleague. I managed to have an argument with some of our fans about Peter Lorimer but I'm not sure why! The Kop was packed as usual, the fans were swaying and there was a fantastic atmosphere. At one point I fell down the Kop when the crowd surged forward and scraped all my leg. I had never heard the Kop cheer so loudly, it was brilliant. When McKenzie scored the goal for Leeds in a 1–1 draw we went absolutely mental, getting hugged in the process of the celebrations. Everyone was jumping about for at least quarter of an hour and I was absolutely shattered. Because the match ended up with another draw this meant a second replay had to be arranged.

25 March 1975 saw the next match in the marathons of playing Ipswich Town in the FA Cup replays which meant a visit to a neutral ground, Filbert Street the home of Leicester City. I went on an Abbey Coachways coach to this, which meant I didn't need to leave work so early. Snowy and some others decided to attack me on the coach and tie my wrists together with my scarves. When we arrived at Leicester the coppers refused to let us into the ground because we were Leeds fans. Eventually we got in after going right around the ground. When going back to the coach we were shouted to by some lads I knew and lots of them had stolen Ipswich scarves. The match ended up with another 0–0 draw which meant a further replay was set for Thursday evening of the same week. This meant there were Saturday, Tuesday, Thursday and Saturday matches in one week. I think football players today would have a fit if they had four matches in a week.

So to 27 March, I got home from work to find out that Abbey Coachways had cancelled the coach due to lack of interest with another replay. Karin ran me through to Leeds to enable me to catch the special again. I was talking to some lads who thought we'd get smacked in as we were wearing our Leeds colours. In the ground stood with the Rotherham, Donny and Northampton lot. They asked if our photos had come out from Anderlecht, which they had. When Leeds scored everyone was hugging each other but we ended up losing the match 3–2 with Clarke and Giles scoring for Leeds.

The Easter period saw us play Sheffield United twice in two days, home on 15 April 1974 then away the next day. We were robbed at the home match and the Leeds fans were going mad. I'm not sure if this was the match where the ref kept disallowing our goals and could also be the one where the Kop started singing, 'There's a bald headed b*****d dressed in black, dressed in black, dressed in black, dressed in black, black, black. Every time we score a goal he tells us no'. At the away match the next day at Bramall Lane, the Leeds fans decided we were going to take the opposition end like we did at Coventry. As we were there early, we all queued up to go in Sheffield's end and there were loads of Leeds fans there. We did this without any resistance from the Sheffield fans. By the time they arrived at the ground their end was full of Leeds fans and they disappeared as soon as they saw us and the coppers didn't even try to stop us going in there. The chants were 'We took the Shoreham, easy, easy'. 'We had joy we had fun we had Sheffield on the run but the joy did not last cos the b******s ran too fast'.

20 April 1974 saw us play our last home match of the season against Ipswich Town. It was packed tight in the Kop and the atmosphere was fantastic. We thought we had won the league that day as we ran out 3–2 winners but it was going down to the last match. We had to come out of the match ten minutes early because the tickets for the last away match of the season at QPR were going on sale straight after the match. What a mistake that was and Leeds soon realised they couldn't put them on sale. It was absolute mayhem in the West Stand car park and we were all getting crushed. A message soon came out that no tickets were going on sale today but would be on sale in the morning. We went up to Christine's house in Harehills for a few hours and then made our way back down to Elland Road for midnight as we were going to queue up all night. We were right at the front of the queue, which became longer as the night went on. It's surprising how tarmac didn't even feel uncomfortable, especially because we were queuing for something so important. There was a brilliant rapport with the fans near us overnight especially as we were all after

the same thing. As soon as the ticket office windows opened in the morning we were amongst the first to get our tickets, but there was still a rush of fans trying to get in front of us.

Sue and I were waiting for the train home at Leeds station in August 1974 on our return from the match at Stoke. A copper told us we would be safer standing further away because our hooligans were coming in on the football special. Unfortunately he didn't see the funny side of it when we stayed where we were and were shouting hello to lots of people we knew when they got off the special.

Travelling to Halifax in March 1977 for the semi-final of the West Riding Cup at the Shay, there were about 30 of us altogether. There were two groups of fans that travelled, some of us who went in the Gelderd End (my friends and I) and others who went in the South Stand at Elland Road. The South Standers tried to start an argument with us saying that no Gelderd Enders goes away, and there were more of them than us. Says it all really when we were on our way to an away match and we are Gelderd Enders!!

One day we went to the Three Legs and sat with the twins, Barry, Jock and one of the Donny lads. There was a raffle and the fella selling tickets told the lads that I was third prize and they could have me for a week and then he wanted me back. Barry said I don't know why you come in here and how you can stand it all. A lot of the time it washes over me but other times it hits me like a ton of bricks and I can't stand it. Collar came in; he'd just come back from Israel. Some lads from Keighley came in collecting for three Leeds United lads who had been killed in a car crash. They were on their way home from a Leeds match at Birmingham and were just a few minutes from home when it happened. I recognised one who was collecting and he said the lads usually came in the Three Legs. Passed Martin, Timmy, Dick and Phil from Snaith going out and they said I'd to go in the ground with them and they'd protect me from the Meanwood lot.

After Leeds were robbed in Paris by the allegedly bent referee, Leeds fans started singing 'We are the Champions, Champions of Europe' which we believe we rightly were. This started off when Collar (he took over from Pedlar and/or Wilkie if I remember correctly) stood on the barriers half way up the Kop and turned to face the back of the Kop with Paul holding on to him to stop him falling off. He then shushed the crowd and then split the Kop in two. One half of the Kop then sang *'We are the Champions'* then went quiet whilst the other half sang *'Champions of Europe'*. It was fantastic and sung like this it had so much impact and the noise was immense. Currently it is sung too fast and it all blends into one chant and whilst the scarf waving is brilliant, I wish we could recreate this scene. The younger fans at Elland Road have never experienced the proper chant and it is awesome in action! By standing on the barriers the lads regularly shushed the crowd to get the fans singing which was fantastic and was something that happened at every match. As soon as you saw the lads getting on the barriers you knew what was going to happen. A number of years later the fans would take their shirts off and wave them around their heads no matter what the weather was like.

The Kop was where all the Leeds fans congregated after the Scratching Shed was demolished and the South Stand built in its place. Where we stood in our regular place at the top of the Kop, it was packed every match with the same people around you. At the first match of the season it got a bit crowded at the top of the Kop so the coppers moved some fans out. We got in at the side and worked our way across the middle of the Kop. It was packed out and loads of lads kept grabbing my bum. I nearly went flying because of all the shoving and pushing and Karen ended up on the floor and I had to pull her up. We got to near where Collar stands and a lad grabbed hold of me and kissed me on the lips then shouted he'd scored. I was flabbergasted, and then loads started grabbing my bum so we stayed where Sean and Collar were. I was saying hello to everyone, Paul, Vince, Ian, Leslie and little Barnsley. Nearly had a fight with Sean's mates as they all kept calling me a hooligan, which I suppose made it look plausible although in reality it couldn't have been further from the truth. It was great to be singing and chanting again and fantastic especially when Leeds scored two in the last five minutes to draw 2–2. The shouting was unbelievable and when Clarkey scored right on full-time we went loony, hugging everyone. We all stood singing *'You'll never walk alone'* with our scarves held high after the final whistle and one lad commented on the fact that I was singing it with such gusto. All of the Kop was singing and cheering and on *Match of the Day* later that evening the Kop looked fantastic when we scored. Went down to join Carole and Sue and met Karen at the bottom of the steps and she said there'd been an accident as all the fans piled down the steps, they'd fallen on top of one another. One lad I'd seen on the Kop was saying what a great fan I was and he'd seen us in the paper. I'm still as mad as ever and Carole and Sue are more respectable as they were not as vocal as me!

Another time when I tried getting in the Kop it was packed, so I went up the back way. A lad from Barnsley was with us so we let him push his way over and whilst following him I got my bum nipped twice. As we got to where we usually stand a lad said don't tangle with her or she'll hit you. Someone kept nipping me so I said if they didn't give up I'd belt them. I don't trust half of the lads as they used the excuse of falling all over the place with the crowd and kept grabbing hold of me. When we scored everyone went mad and I kept falling all over the place with the surge of the crowd. I went up to join our lot at the back of the Kop and someone nicked my hat, it was one of the Goole or Stainforth lot. They thought I'd pinched a hat because I'd got my hands in my pocket and they dived on me and we went flying backwards down the Kop and ended up on the floor and then they had to pull me up.

The 'dangers' of the terraces happened a lot during big crowds especially on the Kop. During one match we scored and I ended up on the floor and when I got pulled up found my knee was soaking with blood. Leeds scored again and I automatically jumped up in the air and then got pushed by the crowd and ended up with the end of the barrier in my stomach and was doubled up in pain. A lad asked if I was okay and when I said yes I'd just got the barrier in me, he said you don't look it. Saw Mick from Selby and Nick who shouted Heidi just as we got back to the top when we scored and I could see what was going to happen. Karen went hurtling down the terraces and landed on her back and hit her head on the step and all the lads fell on top of her. I couldn't stop her and I dived down and got her up with the help of some lads but still fell on the floor a few times. We got over to our normal place and Karen recovered but near the end of the match she said she couldn't see and I said she'd probably got concussion. She sat down in the box at the back but then was okay. The atmosphere in the first half during a different match was magic, especially because at half time we were leading 5–1 and you'd have thought we'd won the cup. Saw Sal and Collar at the end of the match and he said he was going to break our gang up.

On another occasion, I was pushing my way to the top of the Kop. I saw a Donny lad and he made a grab for me, so I caught hold of his hand and he said she's holding hands with me now. Got to the top and they all started grabbing my bum Bob, Kev, Brian, Pete and another lad were all as bad as each other. I caught hands to find out who was doing it and found it was Bob and Brian mainly. They were all coming out with rude things about me and grabbing me. Some of the Selby lot were behind, Steve, Ian and the Hunslet lot. Because it was packed I ended up on the floor with the lads on top of me and had to be pulled back up again. At half-time I sat down to avoid them all and they still pushed onto me and I intended staying sat down when the team came out again but they pulled me back up again.

Left: Hibernian away – Brod and Trev. Right: We won the league – Esther, Sheila, Christine, Helen, Sue, Heidi, Christine and Sharon

Left: Mouse and Dillon at Burnley, 27 September 1975. Right: 13th December 1975 – Kev and Bob (middle and right)

Left: Arsenal 6th December 1975 – Ian at the front, on the coach coming back
Right: Leeds and Man City fans in the Supporters Club – Tony from West Midlands, Jock and Mick

Left: Brod, Gary Noble, Gary Edwards in the Three Legs. Right: Leeds fans in the Three Legs including Dave and Mick Howdle

Left: Leeds fans at Coventry Alan second left, Ian, Alan and Steve on the right

Chapter Eight

Relationship with the Leeds United team & staff

After the Stoke match on 6 October 1973 I stayed in Leeds that night and went down to Elland Road the next morning to see the team training. They were getting prepared for the trip to Ipswich the following day. I was over the moon when both Billy and Les Cocker spoke to me and I told the team coach driver that I was also going to the match.

As part of Billy Bremner's testimonial celebrations in 1974 I went to the Irish Centre in Leeds. My mum took a photo of me getting Billy's autograph when he was sat with Don Revie and Paul Reaney. My mum won an autographed football so I was ecstatic and my sister Karin won a tie. When I went to get autographs Terry Yorath said to me that Frankie Gray had been trying to think where he's seen you before. I said that would be at Elland Road before the Ipswich match in the League Cup. He replied that's it. Terry Cooper also asked if I had come all the way from Selby for this to which I said yes and he said I must be mad! Some lads said I was jammy because I won the football and it was noted that for once I wasn't wearing my Leeds things but was actually wearing a skirt.

The third away trip in a row took us to Birmingham City on 15 October 1974 travelling on the National bus again. On arrival at Birmingham we went into their supporters club before the match. I was chuffed to see Maurice Lindley, Tony Collins and Cyril Partridge (Leeds United's backroom staff) sat behind us in the ground.

Before home matches we had got into the habit of calling in at Terry Cooper's sports shop on the bridge that was not far from Briggate. We used to pass it when walking down to the ground and always called in to say hello.

Terry always had time to chat to the fans though, which was great. Before a home match against Stoke we went into Terry Cooper's shop and were talking to him about the forthcoming pantomime. Leeds United players were going to be in the pantomime Cinderella at the City Varieties in Leeds. Billy Bremner was to be Buttons, Duncan Mackenzie was Cinderella, Eddie Gray and Frankie Gray were the ugly sisters; Norman Hunter was Prince Charming with Jimmy Armfield as the narrator. Joe Jordan, Gordon McQueen, Peter Lorimer, Paul Reaney and Terry Yorath also took part but I can't remember what roles they played.

On the way home from the Arsenal match on 12 April 1975, we shared a train with the Leeds players. We went and stood in with the players until we were chucked out by the conductor. Billy said he was only signing autographs for our lot because we went all over. We went into the buffet on the train for a while and then decided to try and get back to the carriage with the Leeds players in. We managed to get back in without any trouble so we went to talk to the players and got them to sign our programmes. We were talking to Sid Owen and Bob English when they asked if we were going to Barcelona and how we could afford to go to all the matches. Had a long talk to them about having two part-time jobs as well as my main job so that I could follow Leeds everywhere. When we went back to our carriage Sid thanked us for our support.

Although the season of 1975 was over, there were still plenty of matches to see. On 5 May 1975 we watched Norman Hunter's testimonial at Elland Road, which was Leeds v Don Revie's XI. We lost the match 3–2 with Bremner scoring both the Leeds goals. After the match I walked back to the station and when passing the Dragonara hotel saw Norman Hunter and Allan Clarke. Also passed Mick Jones under the bridge who said hello to us and shortly after saw Joe Jordan with his girlfriend who smiled at us.

Our final match before the European Cup final was a testimonial at Walsall on 13 May 1975 for Nick Atthey which ended in a 3–3 draw and goals from Clarke, McKenzie and Jordan for Leeds. There were five of us who went from Leeds. I was talking to the team coach driver and showed him our picture in the paper. Whilst waiting for my connecting train, I had three quarters of an hour to wait on Sheffield station in the freezing cold and a thunderstorm. Got to Leeds at 3.15 am where my dad picked me up.

Met Carole and Linda after the Tottenham match at Elland Road and went out in Leeds afterwards. We went to Nouveau nightclub and Peter Lorimer and Eddie Gray were there with their wives and both said good evening ladies to us when we walked in. We were dancing when Eddie and the two wives came to dance alongside us. Eventually we all ended up dancing in a circle but Mrs Gray wasn't keen on this. I was meeting my parents later on in the evening but the car had broken down, so I ended up staying at Carole's house and went straight to work the next day. Apparently after this the Leeds United Juniors were talking about us at Elland Road and the first team, saying we keep going in nightclubs where the first team go. We're well known now, although we never gave it a thought about being seen as 'groupies' as someone called us. Unfortunately it looks like others see it in a different way. At another match whilst walking up the street we were passed by Terry Yorath, Frank Gray and Gordon McQueen, so we all swooned as usual. For us it was a thrill just to be spoken to by any of the players, sleeping with any of them never even entered our heads.

After we had played man utd at home in 1975 I stayed at Carole's house overnight and in the morning we went down to the ground. When we got there I was mad when I saw that man utd fans had sprayed a lot of graffiti around the ground and I tried rubbing it off with no success. There was no way that I was going to let that stay on the walls around Elland Road as I hated them with a passion. I'm not sure how many of us there were but I think about four or five of us. We then went to see the groundsman who gave us some stuff to clean it off with and managed to get most of it off. On our way to take the stuff back someone said I take it you don't like man utd then, and received a unanimous reply of NO. We went into the ground but couldn't find the groundsman. Peter Lorimer was running around the pitch and Jimmy Armfield and Eddie Gray were watching from the tunnel. Peter said good morning to us. We went over to Jimmy and asked him if he would give the things back to the groundsman for us. We told him we had been cleaning man utd obscenities from the walls of the ground then I asked if there was anywhere we could wash our hands as we were dirty. He was a bit shocked but thanked us and he said we couldn't go in there at the moment as they (the team) were all undressed. Instead he told us to go to his office, so we went in there and washed our hands. Frankie

Gray was in Maurice Lindley's office and he stared at us as if to say what are you doing in here?

We then went to Sheila's café and had an argument with some of the juniors who were in there, but I've no idea what the argument was about. Carole went off to work and I stayed there a bit longer. I then went to the club shop and claimed my commission (which I got for selling bingo cards) and then spent it on a White Leeds Jumper, a Mirror, pennant and calendar. I then went into town and got some Brutus kegs and hung around for a while. Eventually I went to the garage where Terry my brother-in-law worked to get a lift home. We heard later from someone that Mr Sanders and Jimmy Armfield had a long talk about us and he said if all fans were like us there would be no problem. He thinks we are great.

On 22 November 1975 we played Birmingham at home and had a good 3–0 win with goals from Bremner and McKenzie (2). On the train into Leeds I started getting names and signatures for a petition, after Leeds were banned from Europe for four years after the rioting at the European Cup final in Paris. Jimmy Armfield had asked for views from the fans who were there to appeal against the decision. I got a load of names, 73 on our train alone. When Steve Fender got on he started on about Zurich and one of his mates said, shall I put my name and address down? They also said I should go on their coach to Ipswich. I met Sue and Carole in the station and got some more names there. Went for a service bus and saw Pedlar, Bob and Kevin and they signed too. I went to see if my photo album was ready as it was being autographed by the team. Went to the official entrance and got more fans to sign the petition. We asked if we could go and collect names for the petition from the South Stand and we were told we needed the permission of Keith Archer who was in charge of this side at Leeds. So we went back to the main entrance and asked to see him and told him what we wanted to do. He went and got us some official passes and wished us good luck. Started to walk down to the South Stand past the West Stand and the fans there started whistling and singing South Stand boys we are here. Had to climb into the stand but managed to get loads of names, although we did get Donald Duck and Mickey Mouse which was a bit disappointing. Also had someone nipping my bum so I told them to keep their hands off otherwise I would "smash" their faces in.

We climbed out of the stand and started walking along Lowfields Road. The Kop looked fantastic. Saw a steward we knew at the bottom of the Kop and he asked what we were collecting. Started walking across the front of the Kop and saw the fella who wears the top hat and he signed. The Kop started whistling and some lads chanted Heidi from the top then came the lovely chant about t*ts. How we blushed. Saw the Hull lot who signed it and then left the petition with a steward during the match. Got to our usual place at the top and saw Violet so went and stood with her. She said when we were walking across the front some lads were singing *'Heidi we'll support you evermore'*. At the end of the match Carole went to get the team and Jimmy Armfield to sign the petition as Sue and I ran out of the ground. Dillon wanted to sign the petition and said to bring it to the South Stand again next week. As we were walking back down to the station some lads had seen us walking round the pitch and asked us how many names had we collected? The following home match we carried on getting more people to sign the petition and got a load more signatures. Saw some of the juniors in the pub and Linda said that they were talking about us and had got our picture from the *Daily Express*. Jimmy Armfield took our petition with him when Leeds appealed about the European ban, which was then reduced to two years.

After an away match we went to see the players off and as Paul Reaney was getting on the coach I said, "Don't speak to us then". He said, "Hello I'll see you next Monday". I said "hello" to Mick Bates and he said "Hello you get all over don't you". Then Billy (my little hero) came out and I said, "Well played Billy you're playing better than ever'. He said "Thank you love" and looked up and smiled. Peter Lorimer smiled at us and said hello. I asked Jimmy Armfield if they were still playing in Amsterdam and he said yes. We spoke to Bob English and the team coach driver too.

At the last home match of the season at Elland Road against QPR on 14 May 1977, which Leeds lost 1-0, Carole and I went down to present a bottle of champagne to the team that we had decided to buy for them. We went in and asked the secretary if she could give it to the players. She thought we should present it to someone ourselves so went and got Trevor Cherry for us. She asked him if he remembered us? He replied that he thought he had seen us at a 'few' matches! He told us we could present it to all the lads ourselves so we went in the lounge and did that. I said this is to you all from the Leeds fans and I told them to win for us today and score a few goals. Joe told us that they would but unfortunately that didn't happen with them losing – maybe it was too much champagne!!

After a different match Carole and I were going to the Menwith Hill Supporters Club do just outside Harrogate after a home match. We got there at approx 8.00 pm and met some of the Fullerton Park lot. We saw Sharon, Margaret, Roy and Kath (they're getting engaged) and saw Eric and asked where we'd to sit. The Leeds United team always came to this event and mingled with the supporters. We saw the team arriving, Peter Lorimer, Eddie Gray, Frankie Gray, Dave Stewart, Paul Reaney, Tony Currie, Norman Hunter, Terry Cooper, Mick Jones, Allan Clarke, Joe Jordan and Ray Hankin. Later on we saw Peter and Eddie and we were talking to Peter. We saw Eddie whilst standing at the bar and he offered to buy us a drink and said we had to drink whatever he bought for us. It was crème de menth and I made Carole drink mine because I had to drive but I also didn't like the look of it. Keith Archer was friendly and asked us when we were going to get married and we said not for a long time. He said something had gone wrong along the line, as we should have been snapped up by now. I told him I couldn't afford to look after myself never mind anyone else and he said the lad should look after you. Eddie told us not to lead a boring life and get out and enjoy ourselves. Went to try and get some photos of the players and asked Tony for one and he asked who am I having it with, I'll have it with her and put his arm round me. I asked Ray Hankin for a photo and a woman said she'd take it for me and he put his arm round me. I took a photo of David, Paul, Chopper and Norman and Chopper asked where he knew me from. I told him I used to go into his shop and he said I thought I knew you. Whilst talking to Chopper, Joe smiled and said hello, I suppose I haven't totally fallen out with him after all since his transfer across the Pennines. It's great the way we can talk to all the players.

The do finished at 2.00 am. A Leeds lad didn't recognise us out of our Leeds regalia and said we looked elegant. Graham Petch was sorry for an overdue apology and a couple of lads we knew kept glancing in our direction probably because they couldn't get over the way we were dressed.

The rapport we had with the Leeds United team in the seventies is still in evidence today. Whenever we see any of the players at Elland Road or at any events, they always take the time to speak to us. The fact that they remember us is, I feel, mutual respect because we all shared the glories of either following or playing for Leeds United at the same time. They were part of my growing up days and will always be a part of my life, as is my love for Leeds United.

Chapter Nine

Amsterdam Tournament 6th August 1976

The season started with a trip to Amsterdam for a four-day tournament with Anderlecht, Ajax, Borussia Moenchengladbach and Leeds taking part. Total cost for the tournament £75.48.

Sue, Jonathan, Nicky and I went through to Leeds on the Thursday night and we were met at the station by Carole, Alan, Leslie and Ian. We went to the Three Legs first and four of the juniors came in, George Boyd, David Reid, Billy McGhee and another lad called Tony. George asked us how long we were going for. We then went to Carole's house and waited until the taxis came to take us to the coach, which was coming at 4.00 am, to take us to the airport. We arrived at our hotel in Amsterdam – Hotel De Munch about 11.00 am to find our rooms weren't ready. We decided we would go and buy some postcards so nine of us set off, Carole, Sue, Vince, Paul, Gary, Jonathan, Nicholas, Alan and I. As we passed a bar we heard someone shout Leeds and found some Leeds supporters were in there with some Borussia fans. The Leeds fans were Phil from Wrexham and Adrian from Shrewsbury. We sat talking to them for a bit before going back to our hotel to get changed. Sue and I got changed into our shorts and Leeds shirts to go to the ground to buy tickets. They'd taken two and a half hours to clean the room up for us to go in as they'd had man utd fans in the night before.

We caught a number 16 tram to the ground. As we got our tickets these Leeds fans came up and said some others were playing football across the road. So we went across and found infact that we knew the majority of the people who were there. They all kept staring at Sue and me in our shorts and we started getting embarrassed. We then went back to the hotel to change into jeans and have a rest before going back to watch the first match.

We set off at 5.00 pm to go back to the ground. Whilst we were stood outside the turnstiles a fella looked at the badges on my scarf. A Leeds lad said watch his hands, she's not one of those from the red light district she's from Leeds. There were about 2000 Leeds fans there altogether and it was great seeing everyone again. We went through the turnstiles and there was a large walking area around the ground before you went onto the terraces. We climbed over a wall to get to the top of the stand where all the Leeds fans were. We knew most of them and they were all saying hello to us including the Donny lot, Malc and Ian. Went and stood with Phil and his mate from Wrexham and they said I was chicken because I hadn't worn my shorts to the match. Gary Noble and Gary Edwards were stood with us too.

Leeds played Anderlecht in the first match. The Leeds fans then started going across to the Ajax fans and they kept running away. Then all of a sudden they retaliated and came back at the Leeds fans catching some at the other side of the fence, kicking the hell out of them. The Leeds fans managed to get back to our side. Douggie got stabbed in the arm and managed to get on the pitch with Milly from Barnsley. Tin cans were flying everywhere. As soon as our match finished we went because the trouble was getting very serious.

Saturday 7th August 1976

We went to the Schiller Hotel for the welcome party with the Supporters Club lot and met Margaret and others on her trip there. They didn't get out of the match when we did and they and little Sharon had police dogs set on them. They also had glass smashed from windows thrown at them as well as tin cans. Roy got beaten up by the coppers with the dogs, but they didn't go for the proper troublemakers though. A large group of us went down to Ajax's ground to look around but as it was a Saturday no one was there and they told us to go back on Monday. We all went back to town and went for a walk round the shops. We went down the Chinese streets that weren't too bad but up near the central station we went into China Town and the red light district. It was broad daylight but I was terrified because we were being stared at from all the corners of the street. A black man grabbed hold of Sue and said come on to her. She told him to bog off but didn't see the knife he was holding in his hand. We dived down a side street and got out as soon as we could but ended up walking by the side of the canal and saw all the prostitutes sat in windows. We tried finding the hotel where the Leeds team were staying but couldn't find it. We walked miles before catching a tram back and going to the Ajax bar.

Sunday 8th August 1976

We stayed at the hotel in the morning having showers and washing our hair before we went for a trip on the canal and then back to the Ajax bar. Jonathan, Nicholas and I went to find the team hotel again. We walked miles before we eventually found it, I spoke to Jimmy Armfield on the internal telephone after being put through to him and he told us all to go back to the hotel after the match. We caught a number four tram back to town and it was right beside the fountain where we could catch it. After all the walking we had done we only had to walk 100 yards to catch a tram direct to the hotel. We got changed ready for the match and I wore three scarves but took a bag to put them in just in case we encountered some more trouble. As we reached the ground all the Leeds fans were stood outside but not half as many as the other day. Douggie showed me where he had been stabbed on his arm. He was lucky to get away with three strips on it and covered it with a plaster. We heard that some Leeds fans had weapons including a hammer and flick knives. These two lads shouted my name and asked if I remembered them from Castleford, so I said yes. They said they were working over there and said they'd come to the match and they bet the first person they saw would be Heidi and it was. One of the lads came up and said I'd get £25 for them down the red light area, but I didn't realise what they were on about until they said the same to Sue and £50 to Carole and they screamed at them. We went and bought some pennants and then went to go into the ground and these Leeds fans who were stood outside said we'd get stabbed if we went in looking like that.

We didn't stand with the Leeds fans but sat further down the terraces. Nothing happened during the first half but at half-time I stood up to see what was happening. The first thing I saw was the Ajax fans coming through the fence towards the Leeds fans, so I said come on to Sue and Carole and we went to the loos. We just got in there when we heard them charging across the top of the stand. We were terrified. We could see the Leeds lot come running down the steps. When they had all gone past, we got out of the loos and ran round to the side of the ground. We could see all the fans looking over the walls to the outside of the ground and knew there would be running battles going on outside. We got a drink in the bar and then tried getting into the seats at the side of the stand. Eventually they let us in and we saw Peter Lorimer and Paul Reaney who spoke to us. I'm not sure if they were both substitutes, or not playing. We sat on the steps and shouted like mad for Leeds. There were some clever beggars of lads there and the language that one came out with was disgusting. Leeds drew 3–3 but lost on penalties.

At the end of our match we went to the toilets and then I said I was just going back into the ground to see what was happening, where I found the Ajax fans had gone from our end into the Anderlecht end. So I said we weren't going to join the Anderlecht fans now but going to go back to the hotel. We stayed for a few minutes to let things settle down. The Ajax fans had knives, hatchets, chains, sickles, kung fu efforts, clubs with chains and balls on the end. We set off out of the seats and met Phil coming towards us and he said about 200 Ajax fans had just gone in the Anderlecht end. We stood there talking and then heard some fans coming down the steps. We set off trying to find the exit outside the ground and they said English to us but Carole said "nein wir sind Deutsch". We were walking keeping quiet and then all of a sudden all the lights came on and we screamed. It felt like we had just been caught by the Gestapo!

We were so glad to get back to the tram in one piece. We met Peter, Phil and another lad on the tram and Barnsley got on at the next stop. Phil said they were going to the Scottish bar and said to go with them but as it was in the red light district I was too scared to go with them. We talked to them until they got off the tram then dumped our things at the hotel and caught a tram to the team hotel. We asked if the Leeds team had arrived back and the receptionist said they were asleep. I said we'd been in the afternoon and Jimmy Armfield had said we could come back. She then said no they had not got back so we went and bought a drink and then waited downstairs and saw the coach arrive. Frankie Gray knocked Terry Yorath when he saw us and they all said hello when they walked in. Terry came up and said how did it go and we said we didn't like getting chased with hatchets. He shouted Tony Currie over and then they draped their arms around each other. Terry said, "You know Tony don't you" and when we said "yes" he said "These three girls go all over to see us but you won't know that as you haven't been here that long." Then Terry got rude about my boobs and asked if I was going up with him and Tony to show them to them. I said, "I bloody aren't." They got in the lift and said "Aren't you coming then?" so I ignored them.

Talking to David McNiven and said we'd been talking to his 'cousin' Grant in Bournemouth. Eddie Gray came up and told us not to corrupt this young lad and said Carole had corrupted them at 16. Cheeky sod. Glan Letheren bought us a lager. When he brought us a second drink I had a coca cola but the barman gave us an extra drink, which we gave to Dave Stewart. When Tony Currie was getting his drinks he was saying his room number loudly for us to hear but we declined the offers from them. Billy was the only one on cokes. We left at 11.45 pm to get a tram and when we said to Glan and them that we were going he said he thought we were stopping with the boys tonight. No chance. We told them what rotten penalty takers they were and told Byron he played well and he said thanks.

We were giggling like mad on the way back to the tram. We went to the Ajax bar and saw Vince, Paul and Gary in the one next door so went to talk to them before joining the others. When Sue and Carole went back to the hotel I joined Vince and the others in the nearby bar. Jonathan said he saw the trouble outside and watched about six Leeds fans get knocked to the ground but they all got up again. They'd got some Ajax fans before that though. Vince, Paul and Gary were a bit drunk. They said they'd got like that because they were terrified when they saw the Ajax fans' weapons.

Monday 9th August 1976

Went down to the Ajax ground in the morning and saw Bobby Haarms the trainer and he gave us some pennants and we got about four autographs. We had our picture taken on the pitch before going back into town to do some shopping. We made our way back to the Ajax bar and got some ice creams. We then went to the fountain and Vince and the others were already paddling in it. We all took our shoes and socks off and rolled our jeans up to the knees and went paddling with them. We got a taxi to the airport which cost 35 Guilders (about £9.00). I gave Carole 50p as I had run out of Guilders or Gelderds as the Leeds fans called them. Leeds fans had swapped scarves and banners and sold them in the Scottish and Cockney bars. We also did that in the Ajax bar so that when man utd go over again they'll know we've been. Got back to East Midlands Airport at 8.15 pm and these lads shouted Derby and Leicester at us when we got off. Got back to Leeds just before 10.00 pm and went to the Three Legs. As we were walking to the station a lad passed us with his arm in bandages and plasters on him and Carole laughed. He said is anything funny and she said I thought you were a Leeds fan who went to Holland and got done. He said he was a soldier and had been in Ireland when a bomb went off and he'd got flying glass in him. He was a Leeds fan and we stood in the station talking to him.

Apart from all the trouble it had been an excellent trip abroad to watch Leeds in the pre-season friendlies. We had met up with lots of friends and also made lots of new friends. Ian eventually became Godfather along with Sue and Carole as Godmothers to my daughter Michelle. Unfortunately this trip was the one, which eventually started to cause me lots of problems personally. Rumours started going around the Harehills lot saying that I had slept with a player and it ended up with some of them getting very nasty with me. I think a lot of it stemmed from Sue and I being seen at the ground wearing shorts on the first day when we went to buy our tickets. We had been on holiday to Bournemouth and had got our first ever suntan and felt good and never thought of it giving out the "wrong signals" to some of the lads. Also we had been seen at the players' hotel, but that didn't give them the right to add two and two together and make five. We idolised our team and were loyal but that was as far as it went. We did have a drink with the players and the truth is what is written above and I was never alone with any of them.

Left: Amsterdam pre-season tour 1976 – Heidi outside the ground. Right: Amsterdam pre-season tour 1976 – Jonathan, Nicholas, Carole, Gary Noble, Sue and Gary outside the ground

Above left: Amsterdam pre-season tour 1976 – Carole, Sue and Heidi.

Above right: Amsterdam pre-season tour 1976 – Leeds fans outside the ground

Left: Amsterdam pre-season tour 1976 – Leeds fans in the ground Gary Edwards, Gary Noble and Welsh lads.

Left: Amsterdam pre-season tour 1976 – Leeds fans in the ground

Below: Amsterdam pre-season tour 1976 at the fountain – Alan, Jonathan, Vince, Nicholas, Paul and Gary

Chapter Ten

Harehills

A gang of lads who followed Leeds came from Harehills and were quite a force at Elland Road. I got on well with some of the lads from there namely Trev H. and both Alan Js. As time passed I had some of the Harehills lot who absolutely hated my guts including one named Chris A. I don't know why they hated me because I was a very loyal fan who went everywhere. They were also very friendly with some of the Leeds United junior players.

When we travelled to Stoke for the second round of the League Cup in September 1976 we travelled with Tony and the Viaduct coach. On the way back when I got on the coach Billy McGhee, George Boyd (Leeds United Juniors) and Eddie C. from Harehills were on it. They wouldn't let me go to sleep and poured beer down the back of my neck. I had bought George and Billy a coke in the pub and Billy had said he was sitting next to me on the coach back, but when I sat next to Carole, they got very rude and had me in tears. Tony told them off and Alan J. kept looking round at us.

A match that will always stay in my mind was when we travelled to Middlesbrough on 25 September 1976 where Leeds were defeated 1–0 and the trip cost me £5.13. When I got to Leeds I went straight to the market to get a scarf and got soaked in a torrential downpour. I felt as if I'd just sat in a bathful of water with my clothes on. Got back to the station and saw Carole so we went for a cup of tea. Saw little Barnsley, Sandy, Scunny, Alan J. and the Harehills lot in the station. Went to talk to Scunny and Little Barnsley and the Harehills lot asked if there were any spare seats on our coach but I'd no idea. Went down to the Viaduct and when the coach came it was a 45 seater and only 20 of us on it. Tony asked us to see if there was anyone at Wallies who wanted to travel with us so we went down and saw Gary, Ian, Collar, Gadge and Gary Felton's mates. They all had tickets so Karen and I went down to the station and saw the Harehills mob there. I was just going to see Alan J. when one Geordie lad from Darlington asked if there were any spare seats on the coach and we said yes. About 12 came down with us including Alan and Sandy, Scouse and his mates. Once we got back to the coach a load came across the Viaduct car park. They weren't too bad going to Boro and we kept talking to Sandy and Alan. Some of them kept shouting things about boobs; tried grabbing me and I fought them off but they scared me. We stopped at a pub just outside Boro and they kept staring at me and shouting things to me. Some were okay but one started saying that Terry Yorath had f***** me and I hadn't washed since. He made me feel sick and I said, "You might know people who do those things but I don't" and I walked out of the pub. They think they were being clever. I sat at the front of the coach till we got to where the coaches were parked.

On the way back to Leeds we stopped at the same pub as on the way up when Trev came in with three lads who had travelled by car. One lad with him had got hit in the mouth. Trev spoke to me then Carole said she'd seen him earlier on and he'd asked how I was. A lad with a tartan cap came up to me and started being rude and making bad comments, so I told him to get lost and walked out into the other room. We got back on the coach and I was waiting for Carole to sit down when some lads got on the coach, grabbed me and pulled me down on a seat. I fought them off and kicked one up the backside hard and then kicked another. They didn't like it and swiped my Rangers hat. When I got it back my Leeds badge was missing. They were making rude suggestions and saying I could have my badge back if I went and sat with them and did things, but I wouldn't. They made me feel sick and terrified me. A lad came and tried to sit on my knee and I pushed him away and got up, in the process my shoulder hit him in the mouth accidently but I heard his jaw crack. They were a right hard bunch and kept saying things about gangbangs and I know I wouldn't have stood a chance if they had have really started. I don't know whether they'd have done it to the others but I felt sure they'd have got me. They took Scouses trousers off and then tried to get Charlies off but we tried ignoring them.

We stopped at some toilets and Tony's sister got off and the lads were all stood at the side of the road using the grass verge as a toilet, but I was waiting until they all got back on the coach. All of a sudden they all dived into the ladies. Tony went and told them to get out and once they were back on the coach I went. Tony's sister was in the toilets and I asked her if she was okay. She had heard them come in and pulled her trousers up and when two looked over the top she said you're not going to see owt so you might as well go. Malcolm nearly had a fight as we were getting back into Leeds. When we got off the bus at Leeds a few said tara and grinned. I think they enjoyed making me feel uncomfortable and some thought they were God's gift to women. Today had been a very bad day for me following Leeds; it was bad enough having to put up with trouble from away fans never mind your own.

We went up to the Three Legs and Sean, Sally and Collar were there so sat with them. Sally has the same views as us and gets upset at the names we get called. I felt like crying and got really down. Collar said he'd nearly had a fight with a Boro fan and made us laugh. We'd seen him go into the toilets but he hadn't come out for about five minutes. He also said I looked better without wearing my bib and brace. Saw a lad who'd been with Trev and he said hello. Was going to the loo and someone grabbed my arm; it was George Boyd, so I spoke to him and when I came back saw David Reid talking to Maggie and Gill. As George and David were going out they came over to us and David asked how things had gone. George said Leeds hadn't scored today but I was going to score tonight. I asked him what that was supposed to mean and Sean said he'd better not tell me.

All I wanted to do was follow my team, which was like a drug. Once I had made my mind up that I wasn't going to miss a match, I was determined to do this. I am still very passionate about my team, very vocal and always wanted to show who I supported. But I was beginning to wonder if it was worth it as I was sick and tired of all the abuse we are getting, even from our own fans. Then again, I decided why should I be driven away from the club that I love by some 'idiots' to put it mildly. I have made lots of friends following Leeds and these are the ones who really know me. That is what makes me carry on supporting my team, the love of Leeds and the fact that the only time you saw some friends was at the football and I don't want to give that up. Putting it into perspective, it was only a minority of lads, although the stress and fear they put into me was horrendous. I also appreciated the fact that Trev and Alan took time to ask if I was okay which made me realise that not everyone was 'bad'.

The following week when I arrived in Leeds station I saw the Harehills lot were there but I ignored them. When people spread malicious rumours round that aren't true they're not worth knowing. As I was going out of the station I saw Scouse and three mates coming out of the subway so I went the other way. Later I saw the Geordie lad from the Boro coach in the Three Legs, he asked if I was on the coach again next week and I said I'm bloody not. Saw another three lads who'd also been on the Boro coach and they laughed when they saw how wet I was as it had been chucking it down and started chanting Terry Yorath. As we were going into town saw Scouse and the Harehills mob so we avoided them but still ended up bumping into them later on. At the Supporters Club, Chris A. from Harehills came in with Scouse and made some horrible comment to Carole. After the match I caught a bus into town and ran to the station. Saw Sandy and his mate and they said it's a Norwich fan. Then I saw Scouse coming towards me with Collar and two other lads (one a skinhead) so I went to the side of the path to avoid them. They started laughing and Collar said 'it's the virgin' and then the skinhead threw a can of beer all over me. I called him a mucky b****** and said there was no need for that. I heard someone (I think it was Collar) say the same thing. I hate the Harehills, why do they insist on making my life a misery because as far as I am aware I've never done anything to any of them plus we're all supposed to be supporting the same team. I wish they'd get a life because I couldn't understand their fixation with my life. If I want to do something it is up to me and I don't need their permission!

On our way to Norwich we stopped at the services and the coach drivers from number two coach were there and asked whether I was going to the match or going for a drink with them. There was no contest as Leeds won hands down. As I went out to get some programmes a big lad asked me if I recognised the flag he had. I said yes it's from Holland and he said you should know you were there. At the ground there were loads of Leeds fans outside some looking for aggro. Saw both Alan Js, Ginna, Brod, Cockney Whites and loads more who we knew. Went up into the ground and Sandy and his mates came up, grabbed hold of me and wanted to kiss me but I wouldn't let them. Sandy said that we'd enjoyed it coming back from Boro and I said he must be joking because I was scared out of my wits. At half-time went down to the loos and all the Harehills lot were stood outside. The bar was shut at half-time so the coppers sent us all back up into the stand. Saw Trev H. and he said hello to me. Sandy and his mates grabbed me again and I told them to leave me alone. With Karen and me drinking so much, we had to go down to the loos before the end of the match and then the coppers wouldn't let us go back up into the stand. We stood talking to Alan J. and then Sal before the coppers escorted us back to the coach park at the end of the match.

Saturday 20 November 1976 saw us travel to Portman Road to see Leeds play Ipswich. This was the day I found out what I was supposed to have done which made the Harehills lot hate me. Stayed at Karen's on Tempest Road, went to the station to dump my case and saw all the Harehills lot there including Trev H. plus Collar. Just as we were going to the lockers saw Linda and she shouted Heidi and came to talk to us. Went over to see Collar and he said Linda and Steve were going on the coach with the Harehills lot and that I should go on the coach with them then they could have a gangbang. I told him to get lost. Trev said hello and asked how I was going and I said on Wallies and Karen was travelling with the Viaduct coach. Met Carole and we went for a cup of frothy coffee. All the Leeds lads stared at us as I'd got loads of scarves, my Leeds shirt and waistcoat on.

All three of us (Carole, Karen and I) stood on our own at the match. Karen had said earlier that she would go to matches on her own from now on. Saw the big lad from Amsterdam (number 13 Jimmy from Halifax) and he said. "Here's the scrubber from Amsterdam." I said, "I'm not" and hit him. He said he didn't mean it and I said he shouldn't have said it in the first place. (It is ironic how things turn out really. Ever since I got married to one of his friends in 1988, he has been coming to our house for his Sunday dinner every week and is Godfather to my youngest daughter! It just shows I can forgive and forget!) At the end of the match I went to go out and was stood at the top of the steps ready to go down them when Brod grabbed my leg; I nearly jumped out of my skin! Saw the Harehills lot waiting in a gang and both Eddie C. and Trev H. said hello. Got outside and the Harehills lot charged the Ipswich fans and then a fight started near me. Collar came up behind me and said I'd a nice bum and then, "I've been hearing some naughty things about you, can you speak Dutch?" I looked at him mystified, when he carried on, "About what happened in Amsterdam." I said, "Nowt happened so what have you heard?" His reply came, "About Terry Yorath having you." I couldn't believe what I was hearing; I didn't do anything at all and wanted to know who had been saying it! Collar told me, "All of them and I thought I'd be the first." I could have burst into tears, I was so upset that I just marched along in a bad mood and said, "I don't do anything and I still get a reputation for it." Saw another fight.

Got on the coach and stormed to the back and Carole asked what the matter was and I said, "Something I've heard." She said "about Amsterdam?" she'd put someone in the ground straight about that too. They all think I was the only one who went to the players' hotel and someone in Amsterdam has gone back to all the lads and told them I had slept with Terry Yorath, which definitely did not happen. I'm not sure if it was one of the juniors who was friendly with the Harehills lot who were in the bar when we had a drink, or whether some of the players had been spreading lies about me.

The lads sat on the back seat said, "I think someone's going to get killed." Carole had been stood with some nice Barnsley lads and went on about who they knew. They didn't know my name but then said her who wears all the scarves and they see me everywhere. I went down to ask the driver if he could stop and he commented over the mike, that a young lass had been down to see him and he'd see if we could stop. As we got off the coach at the services the driver said it's only because you asked that we stopped otherwise we wouldn't have. The lad, who Carole had put right about Amsterdam, told her that last season all the lads knew us four went round together and no one touched us but that Linda had changed and he thought we might have. Linda had got engaged to Steve and was getting married, so yes she will have changed and there was nothing wrong with that. Alan asked me where I was going, saying, "Well it says Follow me and Leeds United on your back!" One asked if I went to bed with my scarf on and my reply was that my bedroom was covered in Leeds stuff.

On the way back to Leeds the lads started singing *Heidi aggro, Heidi's our leader* and all stuff like that. We had a right laugh and it certainly cheered us up. After telling me they were going to sing songs about me next week, sang they hated me, but it was all in fun. Talking to Ian, Gary, John and another lad all the way home and Ian said he heard the rumour about me at Boro but kept quiet. He heard some of the Harehills saying we've got that tart who got knocked off in Amsterdam on our coach and pointed me out. B*******. I don't know how we got round to the subject but Mick told us that a lot of people think we're a pair of slags, although he didn't believe it otherwise he wouldn't talk to me. I went to a seat on my own and put my banner over me and tried going to sleep. Whilst I was there Carole told them all about Amsterdam. Eventually I went back to sit next to Carole and Mick got in the other seat saying he'd get into bed now as I'd warmed it for him. He said that's another thing he could write down – Chapter 15 for the life of Heidi.

The fact that I'd been accused of sleeping with Terry Yorath by some Leeds fans, which I can categorically state I never did, caused me a lot of stress and grief. It also made me question why was I still a loyal Leeds United supporter when I had to put up with all the unwanted attention from this band of supporters. It was bad enough having all the trouble from away fans never mind your own.

At the next home match I went to the back of the Kop, where I found Collar. I asked if he could find out who started the rumour about me. At the end of the match, Collar told me that I had started the rumours off by being alone with Terry Yorath. There was no way I was alone with Terry Yorath or in fact any Leeds United player! He said he believed me because he knew I was saving myself for him. Went to the Supporters Club and was talking to Mac and Steve about Amsterdam and was told I should have gone to the Scottish bar with them.

Chapter Eleven

Trouble at Home matches

West Ham United were the visitors at Elland Road in December 1972 and there was a lot of trouble in Lowfields that day with Leeds fans fighting and chasing West Ham fans. I only saw what happened from the Kop and our fans were urging Leeds to win. Around this time I started seeing some of the regular supporters around Leeds station when I arrived on the train. A lad in a sheepskin coat, who used to call me Gooley/Selby was one of them.

When away fans came by train to Leeds they were met by a reception committee of Leeds fans, many who congregated at the Scarborough Taps by Leeds station. Plymouth Argyle were one set of fans who came in the FA Cup fourth round and found they were surrounded by coppers to keep them separated and were 'led' by Leeds fans to the ground. Christine from Harehills was a friend of mine and on one occasion she met me at the station when I arrived. I went with her into the Scarborough Taps and this was the first time I walked to the ground.

Playing man utd at home on 18 April 1973 I went in on the train and was going to catch Abbeys coach home. I got in early and was starting to walk to the ground with Christine and Helen when a Leeds lad told us not to go any further than the roundabout as there were great gangs of man utd fans there. I decided that because I had three Leeds scarves on, shorter hair, which made me look more like a boy, was wearing a Harrington jacket and jeans that I would catch a service bus to the ground. Christine and Helen carried on walking to the ground and had been surrounded by them but didn't have any problems. After the match I tried finding the coach home but it wasn't parked where it normally was, next to the railway bridge on Elland Road. I got threatened and chased by some man utd fans, as all the coaches were theirs. I went back to the ground and rang up my dad who then came with Arthur to pick me up. This was one match where there seemed to be more of them than us! The following season we played man utd again at home, which ended in a 0–0 draw as they played very defensively. Looking back it's no wonder really because at the end of this season they got relegated and we won the League. One of my friends got hit by a man utd fan in the station who was quickly arrested for it. There were approx 10,000 of them and they seemed to be everywhere.

On 4 January 1975 Cardiff visited us in the FA Cup. The match ended with a resounding Leeds win 4–1 with Eddie Gray, Clarke (2) and McKenzie scoring for Leeds. When we got to the ground the Cardiff fans were just arriving so we taunted them by waving our scarves. When we came out of the club some of their fans were going past and we got the usual who do we support and did we come from *Emmerdale Farm*. One of them grabbed my scarf and said how nice it was and I told him to get off it. We went into the Pools Office and the staff in there said that they thought we would be amongst them. We walked into the ground and I was given a Cardiff scarf by one of the stewards. There was a lot of trouble in the ground and at half-time five Cardiff fans ran on to the pitch and started to taunt our fans. A Leeds fan then ran onto the pitch and hit one of them. Coppers started chasing them and there was nearly a pitch invasion by both Cardiff and Leeds fans. Saw loads of Cardiff fans getting done down Elland Road when I ran down to the station after the match with our fans. Just before the station one lad in front of us who must have been a Cardiff fan, got jumped on and kicked. Cardiff fans were running for their lives.

For the second week running I ended up where all the fighting was taking place when West Ham were the visitors to Elland Road. Going back to the station I saw the Hull lads mucking about, and then I saw some West Ham fans running and two getting smacked. As we walked back to the station we became part of a great big gang of Leeds fans and was just nearing the station when Fish and Stevie joined us. As it was the Kop's night out I stayed in Leeds station as I had put my things in a locker. I was still stood in the station at 5.45 pm when a large group of West Ham fans came in. They must have been hiding and I was scared as not many Leeds fans were there at that time. Some

Leeds lads came up to me and told me that a West Ham fan had a knife. He was later arrested and found to be in the possession of a fish knife.

The visit of man utd to Elland Road was on 11 October 1975. I went into the Kop at 1.00 pm where the Leeds fans were in full cry and it was packed out. During the match there were ten man utd fans in the corner of the Kop who got knacked and carried out when they scored. I was raving mad when we lost the match. At the end of the match Leeds fans went to chase the man utd fans but I didn't know what had happened until I was told stories later in the day. Saw two pathetic ones who said something to us, so we were well satisfied when a copper swore at them and told them to hurry up. Some man utd fans shouted at us from a coach but not nastily. We did a detour on the way back to town going to Janet's house first. When we caught the bus there were five man utd fans on it that we had seen outside the ground earlier. One of them said that they were going to set one of them onto us, to which I replied, "I'm scared", but they were okay really. Some Leeds lads who stood near us on the Kop waved to us as they went past in their car. Three of the juniors were on the bus and Billy McGee asked us if there had been any trouble because man utd were rock hard. I told him that was rubbish, where do they get those silly ideas from? Then he asked us if we had caused any trouble – as if!

When we got back to town there were loads of Leeds fans coming away from the station and the coppers wouldn't let us go for a bus. Saw Scotty before seeing Leeds fans running down to the market with six dog vans – sirens on – following them. When we eventually got onto a bus two Leeds lads told us that the man utd fans had coppers surrounding them and Leeds fans couldn't get near them, but one ten-year-old Leeds kid piled into them (how true I'm not sure). Went to the Three Legs and saw one of the lads I always give polos to (tall one) and his mates and asked them if they had got any man utd fans. He said one of them had and another kid had gotten a scarf off a lad and when the lad turned round he said he hated man utd, probably hoping they would leave him alone. On my way back to the station a gang of lads came round the corner and one blew kisses to my scarf. There were only two man utd fans on my train going back home. The following Monday there was a 20-minute documentary on the television about the build up to the match and it showed Dillon with a black eye and showed the Kop which looked fantastic.

On 21 February 1976 Leeds were at home to Middlesborough but Leeds lost the match 2–0. It was also a day where I took my cassette recorder with and taped the crowd during the match. Knox got arrested and at the end of the match Leeds fans went Boro bashing. There was loads of trouble at the coach park after the match and lots of Boro coaches got bricked. As we got out of the ground we saw one fella with a cut face and loads of our hooligans everywhere. Saw the lad who had come back from Celtic with us (Sean). As we were walking back to the station through the park, some lads shouted at us to come in number four your time is up. Two other lads walking next to us asked if it was me in the paper and I said yes. He said "and we all chanted *Daily Express* at you at the Stoke match and you ran into the loos." I saw Leeds fans running everywhere and shouted go get 'em Leeds after what had happened to us up there, when we had the worst trouble ever, as the Boro fans had infiltrated the away end of Leeds fans. The train was half an hour late so sat with the Selby lot. In Selby station I had an argument with a Hull City fan in the buffet. Dad came and fetched me because I missed the bus home and we gave Knox a lift when we saw him crossing the road. I asked if he'd been charged and he said yes; a copper had asked him if he'd been charged yet and when he said no they got him for disorderly conduct, kicking a copper's helmet and standing on it. They ripped his shirt and nearly crippled him and all he was doing was jumping up and down.

In April 1976 we went to the Pools Office and then to the Peacock and there were some Man City fans in. More Leeds fans kept coming in and it filled up very quickly. The City fans were mouthing it and then the Leeds fans started singing and the City fans started as well. Then some of them left but the big City fans stayed. Leeds fans then started singing aggro songs and the City fans decided to get out when a beer glass got thrown at them and the beer landed all over a Leeds lad and myself. A Man City fan went to wipe the beer off the Leeds lad who told him to f*** off. The City fans started to move and the Leeds fans shouted get 'em and charged and beer glasses went flying. Another match at Leeds when we played them was on 26 February 1977 in the FA Cup fifth-round, which Leeds won 1–0 with Cherry (Carole's hero) scoring. I rang up Leeds at 9.40 am and found out the match was on so Karin took me to Selby to catch the 10.22 am train. Met Mick and Andy in the buffet and saw Barry Barmby. Met Carole in Leeds station and she said she'd seen loads of City arriving. On our way out we walked through some of the Harehills lot. At the ground we got our programmes and were in the Pools Office and saw some Leeds fans begin to run and I said, "Watch it there's some City coming." About 30 City fans ran down the road at Leeds who ran (they weren't in any gang). I said that I wasn't scared for once so Carole and I went out but the gang had gone past. I gave John and Mick their birthday cards who were sat with some City fans. John wanted to see my photos and showed them to the City fans and Tony from Walsall, then I took a photo of them all. When we walked out of the club with my banner wrapped round my shoulders, we walked through a load of City fans.

As we got into the stand, we saw that some City fans were in the Kop down in the corner and I said that they'd better get them out otherwise there'd be trouble. Just at kick-off Leeds fans attacked them and they ran like hell out of the Kop and onto the pitch and a lot got arrested. The atmosphere was terrific and the Leeds fans' singing was fantastic. At half-time I was sat on a barrier and Vince and Paul told me to sit down, ha ha so funny I don't think! Saw some little lads from Selby with Leeds shirts on. At the beginning of the second half two Man City kids ran over to the South Stand from the Kop and had a go at Gordon McQueen and he went to the City fan and we thought he was going to knack him but they got arrested. The singing quietened a bit but near the end they really got behind Leeds and when we scored in the 86th minute everyone went absolutely wild, dancing and hugging each other. A little lad from Ossett (Mick Smith's mate) hugged me and another lad and Sal did as well. I could have cried with happiness. The noise was deafening then Ian got on the barrier and I said I'd get up but was too scared but I decided to anyway. I got up on the barrier and the Leeds fans looked fantastic. They were jumping up and down with their scarves held up aloft. Saw Benjy from Whitley who waved, John did too, and then saw Mac and Tony on a barrier too. I had to get back up on the barrier four times because I kept falling off and Karen got up too. Someone nudged me and it was Tony Rowe. When the whistle blew everyone just stood there singing. We then watched as there was fighting in the South Stand where City fans tried getting into the seats and Leeds fellas threw them back. Mick Smith and Gary hugged me and everyone was asking what we thought of it and we said fantastic. Saw Tich, the lad with the patches waistcoat, Tony and Mac.

In the FA Cup third-round at Elland Road against Man City in January 1978, they scored twice and Leeds fans were on about invading the pitch. I got crushed against the barrier and was rubbing my bruises when Brian and his mate asked if I was okay and told me to get under the barrier. Some fans started running on the pitch and fighting with Corrigan. Saw Sally get arrested and her bloke get floored by Corrigan, and then came a mass invasion which meant a lot of Leeds fans got pulled onto the pitch by the coppers because they were being crushed. The match was held up for 13 minutes and I sat on the barrier so I could see what was going on. Coppers were beating one lad up (four onto one) and I said to leave him alone and someone said, "well said Heidi". I saw Percy on the pitch plus Ian and Alan (got pulled on because they were crushed). Eventually mounted coppers came onto the pitch and got the crowd back in. I said to Ruth the only thing is Leeds will suffer. When we got a penalty I didn't look and this Welsh lad said I could cry on his shoulder anytime. At the end of the match talking to Gary Edwards and Bev, then Nigel and his mate were on about me saying my t*ts hadn't done any magic today and as we were going out someone grabbed me so I belted him. A fair-haired lad came up and I was talking to him and he said one thing is it'll save us a lot of money.

After a home match against Newcastle we went round to the Supporters Club and saw Adrian and the Welsh lads and spoke to them. From there we went to catch a bus outside the club and Karen went to talk to a steward (with his little lad who used to stand at the back of the Kop and is now in the South Stand) and I stood at the back. About six Geordies passed us going to the coaches and one had blood all over his mouth. Saw some Leeds fans coming back from there and one smiled and said hello. I got talking to a St John Ambulance woman. As we got on the bus four nutters got on and then nearly got off to go fight some Geordies. When we got to the first roundabout four dog patrol vans, three panda cars and four motorbikes put their sirens on and went racing off down Elland Road so we knew there must be some trouble. Saw a few Geordies with some coppers and one lad laid out on the floor and an ambulance going to help him. At the roundabout and the gas works there was loads of trouble. The Geordies came the back way and all the Leeds fans were waiting for them and there were thousands of Leeds there. We got off at Briggate and went to the market where we waited until the copper wasn't looking and then went in. Went to catch a bus and saw Tony get on our bus and saw Sean as the bus was pulling out. He told us later that there had been loads of trouble. Dave had got done and he had been kicked up the arse. He said the Geordies had smashed a brick into a nine-year-old Leeds kid's face and a few other Leeds got done but so did the Geordies. He said that a Leeds fan had a pitchfork and stabbed it in a Geordie's stomach.

February 1977 at a home match against Tottenham, trouble started in the South Stand when we scored. Loads of Leeds fans had gone in there not wearing their colours, which meant the Tottenham fans were not aware of how many were in amongst them. When we scored this identified who supported who and fighting started. The coppers moved the Leeds fans out of the stand and into the home fans' area. This happened constantly all during the match and one time I saw that Sal was with them. Could see a running battle outside the ground at either end of the South Stand. As I neared the roundabout on my way back to the station, I saw an ambulance and saw Cockney Steve, Ian's mate stood there. Saw Jock and Scunny and Scunny asked if I wasn't speaking and I said I was. Got in the station and saw Sal so went to talk to her and I asked where Hoss was and she thinks he's in the nick. Ian, Gadge and Cockney arrived with four Spurs fans; they'd escorted them back to the station after doing them in. Two of their mates had been in the ambulance I'd seen, saying the Harehills lot had done them bad with bricks and cut their heads.

At the start of the 1977 season Leeds were at home to man utd. I was driving to the Queens Hall with two of the Shrewsbury lads who I'd given a lift to; as we got to the motorway we saw all the man utd fans getting escorted by the coppers. Leeds fans had ambushed them and we saw that the group of Leeds fans stretched from there right back to the station. Later I saw Gary the painter from work (a man utd fan) who told me that he got chased all the way back to the station.

Chapter Twelve

Journeys to and from Leeds

After travelling to home matches with Abbey Coachways and then progressing to the train from Snaith, I started travelling from Selby by train to Leeds. This was because the train from Snaith took an hour to get to Leeds, they stopped running early in the evening and only ran once an hour. The good thing was that there were often lots of Leeds fans on these trains. The trains from Selby were a lot more regular as it was the main Hull to Manchester train and it was quicker to get to Leeds. The downside meant that many fans of different clubs also travelled on them.

More often than not there were man utd fans on our train when we got on at Selby. On arrival at Leeds there were always lots more of them getting on the train there to travel across the Pennines. I could never understand what people from Leeds were doing going and supporting them. Often we had problems from them, but once we got the upper hand. When there were some man utd fans from Hull on our train, Sue and I started shouting Hull City at them, which got them rattled and they threw stones at us. They didn't like being teased about not supporting their local team. Another time there were some really horrible man utd fans on. They said the only reason we went to matches was to get shagged. They saw us going into the toilets and one said I hope you get shagged today – Pigs. On my way home on the train to Selby after travelling to Bury away, I was in the unfortunate company of a load of man utd fans which was very nervy as I was the only Leeds fan and as usual was wearing my colours. At Selby station some man utd lads held the door open for me to go through first, well Leeds are better than man utd! Unfortunately for me personally, feeling scared following Leeds was only going to get worse because trouble always seemed to follow where I was. Even though I wasn't physically assaulted again apart from the Doncaster Rovers friendly (see Chapter five) it left me very nervy.

Going home to Selby on the train Flan and myself encountered Sparky (or Skippy as he also called himself) from Goole a man utd fan. Unfortunately this person caused no end of problems for Sue and me. In my eyes he looked like a gorilla, was massive with teeth missing and was horrible. No matter how much we tried to avoid him he always followed us around and was very intimidating. Once when I was sat with Mick in the buffet, Sparky came in and asked me if I knew his sister and who she was going out with because he's a Leeds fan. I escaped his attentions at the station and when I got to the bus stop saw my brother Rolf with his mates and made sure I sat upstairs with them. That didn't stop Sparky as he just came and squeezed himself onto the seat next to me. Then he grabbed my knee and I told him to keep his hands off me. He said I needed a good f******, to which I said get stuffed we're not like Manchester birds we're respectable. He hit me with his programme and said the only one that wanted stuffing was me and I said no bloody way. If he was the last thing on earth, I still wouldn't go anywhere near him, ugh. I was terrified and shaking like a leaf, also with anger when I got off the bus. Steve said to ignore him and I started crying. I went to the pub with them before going home and cried some more. The following week as I got off the bus in Selby I spotted Sparky in the bus bar and he followed me to the station and came and sat by me. I was ignoring him and he said it was funny on the bus the other week and I said it wasn't. He said something about me getting raped and I said no chance, as he'd get smacked first. Sparky started saying things again so I told him to shut up. On the train he tried stroking my hair and said it was only because he fancied me; I got out of the way quick. A man utd lass called us w******* out of the train window once we had got off the train. Surprise, surprise she didn't say anything to us whilst we were on it. Jonathan and I went upstairs on the bus as Sparky went downstairs to keep two drunken girls company. Another day when we were travelling on the train back to Selby we travelled with both man utd and Everton fans. Sparky had sprained his ankle and I must have been mad, because I helped him to the bus. I just hope he leaves us alone in future.

We started having some problems with a stupid Liverpool fan on the train back to Selby who calls us names and he stuck his fingers up at us. When we got on the train we walked back to confront him and said we wanted to know what we had done to him for him to say and do these things. He tried saying what things and pretended he didn't know what I was talking about, so I told him he made me sick and he stood there looking terrified. I just laughed at him. The following week when we caught the 9.15 pm train from Leeds to Selby, we saw we had some Liverpool and man utd fans on the train including the stupid lad again who gave us a mucky look. As we were nearing Selby he came and stood at the door of the compartment we were sat in saying Leeds are rubbish, singing Liverpool and pointing to his red kegs. He couldn't talk properly and we realised he had a problem. Then he came and sat next to me asking if I had a boyfriend, so I said yes Leeds United. He then tried to put his head on my shoulder so I told him to go away. He then jumped up and made a rude gesture at us. We thought he was going to expose himself and we were ready to kick him where it hurts and pull the communication cord if necessary, but luckily he went away. Everytime we saw him afterwards on the train he was making a nuisance of himself and always wanting to fight so I told him to go home. Why he wanted to fight girls for, I just don't know!

After an away match we went to Leeds station and then walked out of the City Bar in disgust as a woman working there moaned about having to serve Leeds fans. I swore as we came out and this fella in front agreed with us and he turned out to be a plain-clothes copper. As the Leeds special pulled in to the station they saw some man utd fans were on a train and some Leeds fans dived on and got them. I was sat in a compartment with Mick, another lad from Selby and Sid a man utd fan and I had a massive argument all the way back.

On our way to the home match with man utd in September 1977, when we got on the train, we went and sat up at the front with some Leeds fans from Brid. They said two lads further back were man utd fans and as I passed them when I went to the loo one called me a slut. I was raging and told the others I felt like smacking one because of what he said and they asked which. As we got off the train we passed them and one grabbed my scarf to look at it and Mick told them not to be on the train going back. Met Carole and Ian in the station and a few other Leeds fans were in. Saw the two man utd fans off the train and

I pointed one of them out to the Leeds fans and said he'd called me names and one of the lads said which one Heidi. I told them and then they started following them although nothing further happened.

After a home match against Nottingham Forest, as the bus was late from the ground I missed my train. On my way back to Leeds station I saw Dickie from Selby and I stopped and asked if he had missed the train as well and he said no he'd met Sid from Selby (the man utd fan). Sid asked if I was going for a drink with them so I said I'd go even though I'd no money but it would waste a bit of time. Went to the pub opposite Rawcliffes and Mick from Ossett and fair-haired John were in. They both shouted hello and Mick had a Forest scarf and said it was easy pickings. I went to catch the 8.10 pm train to Selby and Dickie and Sid came as well. Whilst on the platform three man utd fans got off the train and were talking to Sid and then they saw Dickie's I hate man u badge and threatened him. They didn't bother me though especially as Sid introduced me to a fella as his fiancée, what???? There were two man utd lasses on the train and they only started mouthing it as usual when I got off the train. Saw Sparky so I hid behind a wall and told Sid who I was hiding from. He asked what I was doing then and I said waiting for my bus and he said to go for a drink with him so I did. Went to the Rose and Crown near the Toll Bridge and met Sid's brother (Keith). When we walked in he kept saying I don't believe it, your mother wouldn't believe it. Someone said a Leeds and man utd fan getting married will mean Liverpool kids. I just laughed at them. I told his mate to make sure they didn't point me out at Old Trafford and Sid kept trying to convert me, no chance!!

Chapter Thirteen

European matches

AC Milan – European Cup Winners Cup Final in Salonika, Greece.
Leeds lost 1–0. The referee was later banned for life from refereeing for accepting bribes to fix the score.

On 16 May 1973 I went to my first foreign away match aged 17. By going into the Pools Office regularly I saw the trip advertised and so booked on the three-day trip to the European Cup Winners Cup Final against AC Milan in Salonika, Greece. I spent £46 on the trip and took £8.00 spending money. Chris, Colleen, Gary Edwards, Keith Gaunt, Carole and Margaret went but I can't remember whether they went on the same trip as me, or whether they were on the two-day or five-day trip. I was on my own and remember sitting next to an old chap and his son on the plane. It was a bit of a rocky trip if I remember rightly with us having to keep our seat belts on as we went through a lot of turbulence. The trip is one I will never forget and I cannot believe that 40 years have passed, especially as I am only 35 (it keeps me young pretending!).

Leeds played fantastically despite the fact that the referee was bribed. He gave AC Milan a dubious free kick after five minutes, which they duly scored from. During the match we weren't given any decisions and should have had a couple of penalties. It was looking more and more obvious that something was amiss when the referee ignored decisions that should have gone in Leeds United's favour. Things went from bad to worse when Norman Hunter was sent off for retaliation, but what AC Milan had done to Leeds without any repercussions from the referee was disgusting. During the match there was a torrential downpour and thunderstorm, which culminated in lightning right across the sky. There was no roof on the stadium, and so we were out in the open and got soaking wet through. We sat on the stone terraces and when we stood up the only dry patch was where we had been sitting.

We were told by some of the Greek fans in the crowd that the referee had been bribed and the way they reacted to us getting beaten was an unbelievable sight. The news had been well known around the stadium as the referee had been seen arriving with the AC Milan team. Because of the perceived injustice, the whole crowd cheered Leeds off the pitch and booed the Italians. The Greeks were going mad and tried to grab my banner off me. Eventually when we were back on the coach to go back to the hotel I dangled my Leeds scarf out of the window for one of the Greeks to have. There were still lots of them hanging about trying to get mementoes from the Leeds fans with at least half a dozen fighting for my scarf.

Back at the hotel, all the Leeds fans ended up in the bar. I can remember being looked after by the old chap from the plane and being bought lots of drinks, which I am sure were called "fix". Well they certainly fixed me because I ended up paralytic and singing Leeds songs at the top of my voice in the corridor at four o'clock in the morning. I got back to my room, which I was sharing with a girl from Nottingham to find a lad in my bed so I just walked out again and wandered the corridors singing. About half a dozen Greeks and Leeds fans ended up on the corridor with me and I can remember a Greek nipping my bum so I turned and kicked him as hard as I could and told him to keep his hands off me. I ended up talking to Adrian from Harrogate and a couple of Greeks for the rest of the night. I realised later that I had put myself in a precarious position being drunk on my own, but luckily some decent Leeds fans looked me after.

Recently Robin Corbett a Member of the European Parliament who represents Yorkshire and Humber has been petitioning UEFA for Leeds to be recognised as the true winners of this final. We were robbed and it was proved the referee was bribed. Why this match was never given to us because of this is something that has mystified and angered me ever since.

Zurich – European Cup

The following year, the first away match of our European Cup adventure saw us fly to Zurich on 2 October 1974 for the return leg with a 4–1 advantage from the home match. I swapped a scarf with a FC Zurich fan by the players' entrance as we waited for the team to arrive. Whilst we were stood there someone asked me if I was from Selby and it turned out that he worked at the funeral directors in the village where I was from. He was at the match with his son. Someone else also recognised me from Hampden Park and Germany when I had been watching Scotland. All the Leeds fans stood together during the game and we lost the match 2–1 with Clarke scoring for Leeds, which meant that Leeds went through to the next round 5–3 on aggregate. After leaving the ground in Zurich a group of us went to a bar where Sue and I got a bit inebriated on three steins of lager each and couldn't remember how we got back to the hotel!

Anderlecht – European Cup

Leeds had progressed in the European Cup when they played Újpest Dózsa over two legs. Although I went to the home match I couldn't afford to go to the away leg, as it was only two weeks after we had travelled to Zurich. The next round of the European Cup was a home tie against Anderlecht on 5 March 1975. Went on Abbey Coachways and arrived at the ground late at 7.15 pm and eventually got into the match at 7.35 pm having missed the kick off at 7.30 pm. There was thick fog and I didn't see two of the goals because of this as you couldn't see past the half way line, although I managed to see the last goal. Leeds won by 3–0 and scorers were Jordan, McQueen and Lorimer. Someone wanted to buy my banner for £5 thinking it had been bought not made by me.

On 19 March 1975 came the away leg of the European Cup against Anderlecht and another trip abroad for us to go on. This time we headed for Anderlecht with Murgatroyd's coach from Harrogate. When we got onto the coach we saw Trampas on it who had given us a lot of stick recently so we told him not to make any comments. We had a long trip down to Dover and I felt really ill by the time we got there. When we got on the ferry I took a few deep breaths and then went to sleep. It was a very rough crossing with a force nine gale, which therefore meant there was a lot of seasickness around. Luckily for me, I must have had my share of being ill before getting on the ferry and I was okay. Eventually we got to Belgium at 1.30 pm in the afternoon. We got dropped off at about 3.00 pm and then found a hotel with the majority of the people on the coach.

We got changed and then all met up to go to the match. We set off with everyone going down the street singing, which was great. Went to the Madison Pub where I saw someone I knew who said he thought it would be me causing trouble. I had some Cockneys trying to tell me my life story and wanted my banner but the little lad (who I gave polo's to all the time) said to leave me alone because I was his and he knew me. When we got into the ground we saw Norma plus the Donny and Rotherham lot. One called out to me, fat arse where have you been. It was just like an away league match with all the young lads who we knew there. It was great. We decided to climb over a fence to go to the middle of the stand and thought that Sue had been arrested as someone tried to stop her climbing over. Later these fellas helped us climb over to join the rest of the Leeds fans.

There was a torrential downpour and we got soaked and it was freezing cold. Leeds fans were fighting in the stand near us and we saw loads of people we knew. I had my banner around me to try and keep warm. When Billy scored we went mad and some Leeds fans ran onto the pitch. Before the end of the match some fans climbed over the crash barriers at the front of the stand. I decided to climb up the fence too and got over and joined the others at the side of the pitch, as I wanted to be there to celebrate with the fans and team. It was fantastic because Billy brought the team across to us after our 1–0 win with his goal. After the match we went back to the pub and then back to the hotel to get changed out of our wet clothes. The long travelling finally caught up with us, we were shattered so we went to bed at 1.00 am.

The next day we went sightseeing with Colin, Mapp, Steve and John where we found an English pub and stayed there all afternoon. Eventually some more Leeds fans arrived with Gary Edwards and Gary Noble, John and a couple of others. I had an Anderlecht scarf as I had swapped my Leeds scarf in Belgium. Eventually we all went back to the hotel to get changed and then went back to the pub where Jonathan took some surprise photos of us. Sue got drunk and started to call me names so I decided I wasn't going to listen to that and took off on my own and ran back to the hotel. I realised I shouldn't have done that and got scared when taxi drivers started stopping their cars for me and I had fellas shouting at me. I didn't stop to find out anything and was very relieved to get back to the hotel in one piece.

I decided I was going to have a shower and wash my hair when Colin came back to check I was okay. I'd locked my door and wouldn't let him in, but said I was okay. Later I went for a shower and there was a row of cubicles that were empty when I went in. I heard someone else come in later and I didn't dare come out till they'd gone because I wasn't sure if they were unisex showers. When I went back to our room Steve came and knocked at the door and asked me to go and look after Sue as she was in their room. I went with him and asked Sue if she was coming back to our room. She told me to f*** off so I said the same to her and stormed back to the room. Sue was then sat in the corridor calling me a bitch and other names. Needless to say we are still best of friends all these years later as no offence was taken and all was soon forgotten. You could say it was all down to alcohol!

A lady called Sheila was on our coach so I went with her to talk to some others off the coach in room 98 and played Knockout Whist; a card game. I was dressed in my nightie with a coat on and unbelievably 'red' socks! The red hatred obviously came later! Trampas and the others came back drunk and everyone congregated in room 98 along with Sue who came and apologised to me. Later Sue and I went back to our room where we went to bed and suddenly there was a commotion in the corridor and a knock on the door. I said to Sue not to open the door but she said she wanted to see who it was. With that she opened the door, asked what they wanted and a load of lads piled into the bedroom whilst Sue ran out. They said it was a good job I had some clothes on, laughing as they all went out again as I hid under the bedding. Sue then went for a shower to sober up!

Everyone on the coach got on really well together. The comraderie between Leeds fans is brilliant and I loved the banter between us all. We left Brussels at 4.00 pm and the lad in the tartan trousers gave me a glass as a souvenir. We took loads of photos. We arrived in Zeebrugge and had to wait until 10.30 pm for a ferry so we went to play darts in a pub before writing Leeds United in the muck on lorries. When we got back onto the coach and were waiting to get on the ferry everyone was singing and the coach was shaking, it was brilliant. Then Mick started to strip off so Sue and I looked the other way. On the ferry we were sat with the lads from our coach, I got tipsy but Sue got paralytic again. Whilst I was talking to the lads the conversation turned to asking if I dropped my trousers and why I hadn't taken my dungarees off yet, so as usual I ignored their questions. I was sat on the steps and a lad shook my hand but then nearly pulled my arm off trying to drag me up. Sue lost her bag but luckily Trampas had it.

On 22 March 1975 we were going straight from Anderlecht to the away match at Luton which we lost 2–1 with Jordan scoring our goal. We arrived at Luton at 11.00 am and went straight to the pub where I proceeded to ring home to tell them I was okay. Walked around the ground with my banner on and then talked to some Cockney Leeds fans before I managed to get in the boys' entrance. I was looking for Sue and saw the Harrogate lads so went to see them. Eventually saw Sue come through the Luton end and walk round the ground. I found Violet and Linda and went to stand with them. Trampas started shouting that I'd not heard the last about my nightie. Well it wasn't my fault that Sue let them into the room! I took it in the fun way it was meant though. After the match Leeds fans stormed the pitch and ran to the Luton fans. The coppers chased them back to the stand and then Luton fans came at us so we just stood there. Some Luton fans started singing about virgins because we sang we are the whites. Got back to Leeds at 9.25 pm and when we got off the coach someone shouted see you Tuesday girls. Whilst in the station I stood talking to Trampas and also Andy and others from Rotherham and Donny. They all shouted it had been great in Belgium. My brother-in-law Terry picked me up from Selby and I got home at 11.45 pm. What a great four days!

Barcelona – European Cup Semi-Final

For the next round of the European Cup Leeds were drawn at home to Barcelona for the first leg. To get tickets for this one you had to queue. I arrived at 5.00 am and pushed in by joining some friends in the queue just outside the South Stand. If I would have had to go to the end of the queue it stretched all the way down Lowfields Road. The ticket office didn't open until at least 9.00

am so we had a long wait. Because there were so many tickets available for this home leg the queue was quite orderly and we had no problems when the ticket office opened, although it was great to know you had purchased your ticket.

The day dawned for the Barcelona match on 9 April 1975 and I went in early on the train. This meant working my dinner hour and leaving work to catch the train. We won the match 2–1 with Bremner and Clarke scoring for Leeds, but Barcelona had a vital away goal, which would count double for the second leg. Before catching my train home I stood talking to some Leeds lads from Kettering and Newcastle in the station.

23 April 1975 saw the European Cup semi-final second leg against Barcelona. We drew the match 1–1 with Lorimer scoring for Leeds and McQueen being sent off, which reduced Leeds to ten men for a long time in the match. Sue stayed at my house and we both got a lift into Leeds with Jonathan. We flew to Spain by travelling on the Pools Office trip and the total cost the trip including spending money was £82.05. After a good flight we had our photos taken when we arrived which cost us 75 pesetas. We got to the hotel and dumped our stuff before going for a walk (Steve, Steve, John, Geordie, Andy, Barry, Sue and myself). We went to get something to eat but I ate very little as I didn't like the food. We then went back to the hotel to get changed before going out on a pub-crawl. I got tipsy and Sue and I had to carry Andy back to the hotel. We stayed in the hotel bar, then at 10.15 pm Sue drank a bottle of wine to herself, I didn't like the taste of it so didn't have any.

I left the others in the bar and I went to bed at 10.30 pm because I was tired, but was woken up half an hour later and asked to go and look after Sue as she had been sick everywhere and flaked out. She tried getting up to go to the loo but collapsed on the floor and was sick again. I had the lovely job of cleaning this up and complained that I always ended up looking after Sue. In the end I took her bag to look after and left a group of them together who were all being sick. She came back to the room in the early hours of the morning worse for wear. After early morning baths the lads called for us on the way to breakfast before we headed to the ground for a look around. It was four miles to the ground and boiling hot. We bought some souvenirs and then got a taxi back to the hotel. Then we spent an hour on the hotel roof sunbathing and swimming in the pool, which was really nice.

We got changed and then headed back to the ground about 5.30 to 6.00 pm. We had a great taxi driver who supported Valencia and he said Barca three Leeds four and shouted all sorts out to the Spaniards as we neared the ground. I bought a scarf and then we walked round the ground and found a load of programmes just left there. I only got a few but we missed a good chance here as these programmes ended up being worth £10 each and we got them for free. We met some Leeds lads and then halfway round the ground met them again, we also met some more who said we had stood in front of them in the ground at Belgium. It took ages for us to find the correct entrance to go in which was right at the bottom of the ground but we were right behind the goal. It was a fantastic ground to be in and the noise from the Spaniards was immense. There were some Leeds fans to the right of us in the next stand and I wanted to go and join them but Sue wouldn't. There was also a small group to the left of us. We got really scared during the match because the Spaniards started getting really wild and started attacking a small group of Leeds lads in front of us for nothing.

When Peter scored our goal we went absolutely mental and then I sat down and cried. It got to the stage that we couldn't watch the match as we were so nervous and found the pressure was so immense, that Sue and I sat with our backs to the pitch. We were reassured by some Barcelona fans that Leeds were going to win, which they did! Leeds won on aggregate 3–2 and it was a fantastic feeling at the end of the match to know that we had got to the European Cup Final.

Billy bought the lads over to clap the fans once the final whistle had blown but we were absolutely terrified of what the Spaniards reaction would be at the end of the match. We tried leaving and then doubled back and went back into the stand. In fact the Spaniards were actually friendlier afterwards than they had been during the match. On leaving the ground we saw two National Coaches and all waved like mad at our fans. We saw Don Revie at the ground as well as Cruyff before getting a taxi back to the hotel and meeting up with the others from our group.

We went out into the street singing and shouting and still wearing our Leeds things and I was wearing my Leeds dungarees. We ended up in a bar where we didn't stay long as it was full of people with missing fingers, dwarfs and beggars and it seemed a very weird place. Sue got attacked by a fella wanting her scarf and a woman tried molesting me so we soon left by taxi to go back to the hotel as we were so scared. Sue stayed down in the bar whilst I went to bed.

At 5.00 am in the morning I heard a banging on my door and Steve (Chinky) was saying the coppers were after him and could he come in. I refused and told him to go to his own room. Eventually everything went quiet and he went away. Sue didn't even call for me in the morning so we ended up falling out. We all went shopping but they left me so I walked back to the hotel on my own. We eventually made up and when we got back to Barcelona airport we were all singing and it sounded great as it echoed. I was glad to be going home and when we got back to Luton we all got on the same coach back to Leeds, which took ages. We got back to Leeds to find out that we would only be getting 8,000 tickets for Paris. I couldn't believe it. In the first place we were told that the European Cup Final was to be held at Hampden Park then it felt that as soon as they knew Leeds were getting further in the competition that it was changed to Parc de Princes in Paris. If it had have been held in Scotland we would have got loads of tickets.

Paris – European Cup Final

Whilst the league matches were still going on, the preparations for the European Cup final in Paris were taking place. Fans were told they had to send their tokens in from their programmes to be eligible for a ticket. Because there were only 8,000 tickets and demand was high it was going to be a lottery but I never dreamt for one minute that I wouldn't get a ticket as I had been to 69 matches that season and Paris would be the 70th. Sue and Carole rang up to say they had both got their tickets but I received a letter from Leeds. I was devastated to be told that I hadn't got a ticket and that the consolation was that it would be screened live on television and I could watch it there. No way on earth was I going to watch the match on television because I was going to Paris with or without a ticket. I had been to all 69 matches and deserved to go in person.

The *Calendar* programme on TV kept featuring fans crying for tickets who I'd never seen before and I decided I was going to contact them. Before

I did that though, a group of us were featured in the *Evening Post* because we had spent £400 following Leeds that season and couldn't get tickets even after going to all the matches. I was going down Mill Lane on my way home from work when my mum came running to meet me to tell me I had got a ticket as Carole had got two. I broke down in tears and couldn't believe my luck. I rang Carole who told me she had applied for a ticket with her tokens and got one but also because she was a season ticket holder she had been guaranteed a ticket so got two. Her unselfish act meant me and Dave Howdle, one of the twins ended up with her spare tickets. I could really celebrate the fact that I was going to Paris now.

We decided we were going to travel with the Pools Office again and once our travel was confirmed found out that we would be guaranteed another ticket with them because we had travelled to Barcelona with them. I decided then and there that I would take the extra ticket and sell it to a Leeds fan in Paris because I was sure there would be plenty there without tickets. Wallace Arnold also ran a coach trip before the match for Leeds fans to go and buy tickets direct from the ground in Paris. Andy from Rotherham was pictured in the *Evening Post* on his way to get his ticket.

The day dawned and 28 May 1975 is a date that would be forever etched in Leeds fans' minds. We set off for the final of the European Cup at Parc des Princes in Paris, Leeds United versus Bayern Munich. We got to the airport at 9.15 am and flew at 10.00 am to Beauvais Airport, Paris. Coaches took us direct to the hotel but the journey lasted about an hour and then we had to wait one and a half hours whilst they sorted out our rooms. As soon as we were able we dumped our stuff in our rooms and then went straight to the ground on the Metro as we wanted to savour the moment. It was very easy to get to the ground and an American woman asked us if we were jigging school. When we got off the Metro there were some Bayern fans so Sue and I started singing. We were stood outside a café when Sue and I were attacked by the Harrogate lads saying here comes the best two girls in the world. We should have travelled on the coach with them to the final because we felt we had missed out on a lot of the atmosphere and build up to the match by arriving late.

We walked to the ground and kept walking around the stadium until we met Carole and the rest of our group. We met loads of fans we knew and a lot asked if I'd got a ticket spare. Some said they'd seen me in the paper. Met Steve and quiet Pete and Sue sold her spare ticket to Pete for £5 (he insisted on giving her more). I met a lad I knew and sold mine for £2, face value to him. I saw the little lad with all the badges and I told him that I saw him get arrested at Liverpool. Met up with the Harrogate lads again who asked why we hadn't gone on Mutrgatroyd's coach and then saw Trampas who said we were hooligans. Got 'attacked' a few times by Leeds fans when walking round the ground and had our photos taken loads of times by German and Leeds fans. I took some photos of Leeds lads with banners and some said there's some Gelderd Enders.

When we got into the ground we were in the top tier behind the goal and my seat was right on the front row next to the clock on the scoreboard end. Saw Dale and others from Whitley sat near us, also Mick, Geordie, Collar, Ruth and Jake. Everything was going perfectly and the Leeds fans were fantastic. The Bananarama song, na na na na, na na na na, hey hey hey, Leeds United was sung for the very first time and it sounded brilliant. Peter Lorimer scored for Leeds in the goal at our end and we went absolutely mental, saw that the referee had pointed to the half way line and were ecstatic. All of a sudden we saw Beckenbauer complaining to the referee who went to talk to the linesman. We couldn't believe it when he disallowed the goal for Billy being offside. We were robbed, especially when Clarke was brought down in the penalty area and the referee said play on. It was exactly the same as Salonika, history repeating itself especially when Bayern scored two goals to win the match.

Leeds fans started rioting and seats were broken and missiles were raining down onto the pitch behind the goal. I went hysterical and then went to join Sue and we cried our eyes out. We were so mad we hit our seats with our banners once but then decided it wasn't the right thing to do. Carole managed to get her banner back, which she nearly lost but I saw it and told her.

At the end of the match Sue, Andy and I went round to the players' entrance where we saw Joe Jordan and David Harvey and asked them why the goal was disallowed and they told us offside. One fella called us stupid for crying, which was like a red rag to a bull and I swore at him and I told him where to go. Saw Trevor Cherry who said all that way for nothing which set us both off crying even more. Eddie Gray gave us a sick smile and we also saw

Don Revie go past us. Don Revie, although no longer manager of Leeds, still had to be there to see Billy and the boys play in the European Cup Final. Andy shouted to Don and asked him to tell Sue and me how Leeds had played and he looked at us, (both still crying) and said they played well. He must have thought we were mental. Then we heard Linda shouting us and we started crying all over again.

Then we went and sat down at a café next to the Metro. We didn't see any trouble after the match just a bit of broken glass but had been told that some cars had been overturned. Dave hadn't been sat with the Leeds fans and said our end had looked fantastic. We were going to walk Linda and two lads who had travelled with Wallace Arnold back to the coach, but someone said that some people were going round stabbing Leeds fans so we got the Metro at 12.20 am and went back to the hotel. After dumping our things in the hotel we then went down the street to where our lot from the hotel were. Saw Mark who said I had brought him a programme back from Zurich and he said he had seen my picture in the paper. Went to bed at 2.30 am and then got up at 7.30 am for breakfast as we couldn't sleep. We then went shopping and bought a paper when a copper came up to us and said we had had bad luck the night before. I thought things couldn't have been as bad as what was being made out with the trouble, if he was talking to us like that. Back at the airport Snowy said a fella had nearly hit him but he pointed to me and said look that lass has been hit over the head and has a bandage round her head, this was actually my tartan scarf.

Afterwards it was alleged that Michel Kitabdjian the French referee had been bribed again just like Salonika, he was awarded just two points out of 20 by UEFA for his handling of the match but no further action was taken against him.

When we got back to Leeds we caught a bus into the city centre and were just going along Boar Lane when the team passed us on an open top bus. Billy turned round and waved at us so Sue and I started crying again. We were talking to a copper after this who asked us about the trip and told us where the reception was being held. We saw Leeds fans going to City Square so we went and joined them. From there we went to the Black Lion where we talked to Pedlar and Paul and some others before we caught the 9.18 pm train from Leeds to Selby. I had rung up home from the station and my dad said my mum had had to have an emergency operation after a routine operation went wrong. She had to have three pints of blood, they couldn't feel her pulse and we nearly lost her. That set me off crying again. I was just so glad that she had come through this.

Later John said my banner is on the European Cup Final film he sent away for and Sue and I should go to his house and watch it. We eventually went to watch it after Notts County in the FA Cup and saw my banner on his films from Paris.

Left: Greece European Cup Winners Cup Final in Salonika 1973 – Keith, Chris, Gary, Colleen. Right: Zurich 2nd October 1974 – European Cup

Left: Zurich 2nd October 1974 – European Cup Heidi, Sue and Roy. Right: Anderlecht European Cup 1975 – on Murgatroyd's coach

Left: Anderlecht – European Cup 1975 – Leeds fans from Murgatroyd's coach
Right: Anderlecht European Cup 1975 – on the ferry

Left: Barcelona European Cup 1975 – Heidi and Sue with banners. Right: Barcelona European Cup – Heidi and Sue with scarves

Left: Barcelona European Cup 1975 – Leeds fans. Right: European Cup Final 28th May 1975 – Trampas, Pete and others Murgatroyd's coach

Left: Paris – European Cup Final 28th May 1975 – Sue, Carole and Heidi. Right: Paris – European Cup Final 28th May 1975 – Leeds fans

Left: Paris – European Cup Final 28th May 1975 – Leeds fans. Right: Paris – European Cup Final 28th May 1975 – Leeds fans

European Cup Final 28th May 1975 – Leeds fans shows my banner stick on front row to right of the clock

Chapter Fourteen

Pre-season friendlies 1977

On 3 August 1977 we set off on our overseas travels to the pre-season matches in Odense, Denmark Cost £73.20 and PSV Eindhoven, Holland Cost £60.00.

Odense, Denmark – Leeds won 4–1 with goals from Lorimer (2), Hankin and McNiven.

I went in Margaret's car, along with Carole, June and Sharon and was to share the driving along with Margaret. We set off from Ramsgate on Friday 29 July and camped on the beach at Calais for the night. We stayed in Duisburg on Saturday, Hamburg on Sunday and Monday, Kiel on Tuesday, Odense on Wednesday, Hamburg again on Thursday, Friday at Marg and Les's house, Saturday in Eindhoven station.

On the way up to Denmark we saw the Fullerton Park branch of the Supporters Club in a village so we stopped the car and they all came running up to see us. We carried on to Odense and ran out of petrol as we had a faulty fuel gauge. We finally arrived at the hotel where the Fullerton Park branch were staying and parked there. We got a lift to the ground with them and had to pay but it was easier that way. We arrived at the ground and Eric Carlile had managed to get complimentaries for his group. We had to pay 18 Krone (£1.80) to get in. Stood with the Leeds lot, there were about 60 of us, including the Halifax lads, two of the Cockneys (Simon and his mate), Collar and Angie. We nearly had some trouble with some lads and Simon and his mate said they would sort them out if they started on me. The match was quite good especially as we banged four goals in.

After the match we went back on the coach as we had arranged but Margaret and Sharon didn't. We were supposed to be sleeping in the car that night and as Margaret had the keys to it, we had to walk the streets, as we had nowhere to go. June had been crying. We saw Esther and Ellen and went with them to look for the others and they bought us some chips and refused our money. We passed the hotel where the team were staying and saw they were there so we went in to see them. Trevor Cherry, Paul Reaney, Paul Madeley, Dave Stewart, Jimmy Armfield and Don Howe were there. Paul Reaney asked how we were getting on and we said rotten and asked about tickets for the Eindhoven match. He said to ask Jimmy who said he would get us some and he'd give them to Paul. Saw Gordon and Joe and Gordon said hello and grinned.

Carole and I then went to look for the others and met June and Mick and we all stood by the car talking when more of the Fullerton Park branch came up Alan, Dave, Chris and Phil and then the Halifax lot turned up. We eventually met up with Margaret, Graham (her boyfriend who we didn't get on with) and Sharon in a disco. We wanted the keys to the car as I was going to sleep there and Carole and June were going up to the hotel. That didn't happen and Carole, June and I all ended up in tears stood by the car. Phil and Alan (from Morecambe) came back to see us and told me to leave a message for Margaret and Sharon on the car windscreen and said we were all going back to the hotel. They smuggled us into the hotel and there were nine of us in Alan and Dave's bedroom. They gave up their beds for us and said although it may damage my reputation it would do theirs the world of good. It was quite funny in the end and we talked for most of the night.

The next morning we were travelling back to Kiel but the car kept breaking down and we had to be pushed over the German border with the help of Jimmy 13 and the Halifax lads. Because of this we were supposed to be keeping up with the Halifax lads but Margaret put her foot down and said we were going too slow. We went to visit my Aunty Anneliese in Kiel and then travelled to Hamburg to see my cousin Rosi. We set off from Hamburg on Friday afternoon and were on the motorway when we got stuck in a traffic jam and the car conked out and we had to get out and push.

A lorry driver stopped and then an army bloke stopped and we pushed the car 1,000m to a parking place and called the AA out. They came but didn't do anything to mend it but put four cans of oil in. We got going again and

Margaret took a wrong turning and whilst we got off the motorway and tried turning round the car conked out again. We pushed it down to the end of the motorway and onto a slip road and a car turned round and a man got out and asked if he could help. It was Les who was with his family Marj, Jan and Paul (he was also in the Army) and Les spent an unsuccessful hour trying to get the car going before they towed us to their house and put us all up for the night. That was a fantastic gesture inviting five strangers into their home. The next morning Les spent two hours on the car before he got it going. I drove from there and we got as far as Duisburg when all the power went out of the engine and I pulled into the side and put it into first gear and it went again so we carried on. Got to Venlo the Dutch border and it conked out again so we had to push it over the border and then got it going again.

PSV Eindhoven, Holland – Leeds won 3–1 with Lorimer, Hankin and McNiven scoring for Leeds

We managed to get as far as Eindhoven and as soon as I changed gear it conked out again and it wouldn't start at all, so we pushed it two miles into Eindhoven and got a tow the last bit to the motel where the Leeds United Supporters Club were staying but they had already gone. We called the AA out and they said it would be Monday before they could get it mended which was no good for Carole, June and myself as we had to be back in work by then. Carole rang her dad up and he booked three of us onto the ferry from Rotterdam to Hull. So we got changed and June, Carole and I got our things and got a taxi to the ground. Saw two of the Telford lot Paul and another, Steve from Shipley and Keith from Morecambe. They helped us carry our bags to the supporters' bus and we left them on there during the match. We went to the players' entrance just as the team arrived. Gordon grinned and waved and Frank Gray had a grin all over his face. Arthur was looking at our Scottish banner and I asked Paul about tickets and he said he didn't have any so we asked Don to ask Jimmy for some. That was the last we saw of them. The only one who came out was Trevor Cherry and he had some tickets and gave them to a foreigner.

At that point we could have cried because the match was already sold out of tickets because it was the opening of the new ground and none of us had been aware of this. We had come all this way to watch Leeds and couldn't even get in the ground. Just then Bobby Robson, manager of Ipswich came out and we asked him if he could get us any tickets and he said "Why can't you get any?" and we said they were all sold out. He went back in and came out with some tickets. We had to pay for them but we were so grateful that we could get into the match and a very big thank you to Bobby for being the only one who cared. We went into the ground and stood with Collar, Angie, Alan, Dave and the other Leeds lot. Saw the Halifax lads and Jimmy 13 came up and gave me a kiss on the cheek and saw Simon with a few more Leeds fans.

At the end of the match we went back to the coach and got dropped off at Eindhoven station. We went and dumped our things in lockers and then went for a drink where we saw a couple of the Harehills lot and one pointed and smiled, they were the decent ones we knew. After we'd had a drink we went for a walk and then came across some Leeds fans outside a bar. Alan and Dave were there and they cheered when we went across. Kev from York shouted "Hello Heidi, how are you?" and the next thing they started singing Yorkshire birds are best. Alan and the others went back to their coach and we went back to the station and were talking to Collar and Angie. Collar went to have a word with the coppers to see if we could stop in the station, which gets locked on a night. We got permission to stop in the waiting room as it wasn't safe for lasses to wander the streets, because it was the red light district just outside the station where all the bars were. Simon stayed with us as well. It was very uncomfortable trying to sleep on the chairs, in the end I put my banner on the floor and wrapped myself in it to keep warm and went to sleep.

Next morning we got up at 6.00 am and caught the train to Rotterdam. We went for a coffee then got some more money changed when I cashed another cheque, before catching a taxi to Europort and spent up there. We were there for 11.00 am and we didn't board until 5.00 pm. On board the ferry we made pigs of ourselves eating and then felt sick. We had a sleep in the recliner seats and then June and I went to the disco. We got chatting to some scousers one Everton and one Liverpool fan, we were talking to them for ages and they said we were real fans. I thought we would get to Hull on time but then we couldn't dock for four hours because the lock had broken. When eventually we got off the ferry I was stopped by customs and had to open my cases, which delayed us a bit more and when I got out to my dad

I was nearly in tears. Got to work eventually at 11.15 am and I should have been there at 8.30 am.

Racing White Daring Molenbeek, Belgium on 12 August – 2–2 with 2 own goals. Cost £20.45.

We set off from Leeds on 11 August, my birthday. I went through to the club at Drax first and was bought a load of drinks before dad took me through to Leeds. I was still dressed up when I got on the coach and they all wanted to know the meaning of it and I said it was my birthday, so they all sang happy birthday to me. We were travelling with Mick Hewitt's coach. I slept a lot on the way down. The crossing wasn't too bad and I got changed on the ferry. There were some lads from Scarborough, Halifax, Alan from Bradford, Steve from Shipley, Keith from Morecambe, and South Kirkby on the coach. We arrived at Racing Whites ground at 1.30 pm but they weren't selling tickets until 2.00 pm so we waited there. Saw Simon (Cockney) and the Halifax lads. Then we went into Brussels and parked the coach there before making our way back to the ground. We went into a shop and everyone had disappeared except Timmy (club shop), Steve, Carole, Keith, myself and one more. We decided to go to the station and met an English bloke who showed us where to get a bus from to the ground. We got off near the ground and started walking up and saw some Leeds fans in a café so we went to join them. Gary Noble, Gary Edwards, the Howdle twins and the Halifax lads were in with some others. We were brought a drink as today was Carole's birthday. We stayed there for a while, then went up to get programmes and went into the Supporters Club. Carole and I both got lots of birthday kisses.

We went to the ground and heard some of the Halifax lads had been arrested before the match had even begun including Ginger Jimmy, for being drunk. Captain had gone to the loo and when he came back Jimmy 13 and a lad from Queensbury had also disappeared. Jimmy 13 got arrested later on. They were all reunited the next day when they returned to the car to find Captain asleep underneath it. As we went into the ground we saw Kaz, Cheesie, Julie, Collar and Angie and some of the Harehills (including Chris A.). Some of the Leeds fans went over to the side where the Belgium fans were and we were going to join them until someone said they were going to cause trouble, so a lot of Leeds stayed where they were. Some Leeds fans ended up fighting with riot squad coppers. Saw Gary N. get arrested and heard Collar got arrested when he was trying to stop the trouble. Saw one lad John come away with a swollen black eye, which looked terrible. All the riot squad were coming in on either side of the Leeds fans so we took off at 9.30 pm to avoid any trouble.

Alan was drunk and we had to drag him back to the centre. We were panicking because we had left our passports on the coach and we had been told later on that we could be fined 500 francs on the spot for not having them with us. Went and had something to eat before getting back on the coach. Went to sleep on the way to Ostend and woke up to a funny smell to find out that Alan and another lad had been sick on the floor behind our seats. In Ostend we had to wait one and a half hours so Steve, Timmy, me and a couple of others wandered around and ended up in a bar where I got a souvenir glass. If we'd gone down the main street we'd have met up with the Leeds lot but decided to avoid it in case there was any further trouble.

We went back to the coach and fell asleep and woke up to find we were on the ferry. So I found a seat on the ferry, put my banner over me and went to sleep only to wake up with a jump at ten to seven when a lad went past and mentioned my name. Went back to sleep and woke up at 9.00 am and had decided I was going for a cuppa only to find out we were docking. Slept most of way through London and passed scousers (Liverpool) and man utd fans going to the Charity Shield at Wembley. Stopped at Scratchwood and some man utd fans came in and one was wearing a I hate Leeds badge. Slept most of the way back then got off at Leeds station for the train. Alan kept saying we'd never forgive him for last night.

Angie, Collar and
Carole at Odense

Leeds fans on Mick
Hewitt's coach to
Molenbeek

Leeds fans on Mick Hewitt's coach to Molenbeek

Leeds fans outside bar in Molenbeek

Chapter Fifteen

Trouble at Away matches

Abbey Coachways ran a coach to the matches at Coventry and Nottingham in 1971. At Nottingham I wore a six-foot scarf that I had made. I was quite naïve to the fact that there may be trouble at matches at this stage. We were followed into Nottingham by a couple of Wallace Arnold coaches. These coaches had a middle door as well as one at the front and Leeds fans kept opening this door and hanging out of the coach. Going back to the coach after the match I hid my scarf under my coat, with a bit of difficulty I might add and probably looked six months pregnant! As I was going across the bridge over the River Trent I was in the middle of all the Forest boot boys who were looking for Leeds fans. It was the first time I had really seen anything like this but I was laughing to myself as I was a Leeds fan in the middle of them and they didn't know it. Once back on the coach, I began to hear stories from the other fans on my coach about the escapes they'd had. We heard that a Leeds fan had been forced to swim the Trent and another had been stabbed in the back and collapsed onto the steps of a Wallace Arnold coach. How true these stories were can only be confirmed by people who were involved.

The second leg of the UEFA cup took us to Hibernian on Wednesday 7 November 1973. This meant a day off work to travel to Leeds in time to get the coach to Scotland. There was only one Wallace Arnold coach that went that day with approximately 25 supporters on it. Sue couldn't go to this one so I went on my own. This wasn't a problem for me because the more matches you went to in succession meant that you got to know the regular fans that travelled to away matches. There was always a lot of banter and we all got on well with each other. It's funny, but the thing that sticks out in my mind is the

Carpenters, *Top of the World* being played at half-time and I was singing it at the top of my voice.

The match was a 0–0 draw after extra-time and went to penalties. By scoring all ours and I believe Billy Bremner scored the decisive penalty, Lorimer, Clarke, Bates, and Frank Gray got the others, we got through to the next round. I swapped my Leeds scarf with a Celtic fan and yes, we were playing Hibs and not Celtic!! At the end of the match we were edging out with the crowd when at the other side of the wall you could hear Hibs fans singing they were going to stab any English b******s they saw. Luckily we managed to avoid them and got back to the coach in one piece. As the coach set off after the match we had stones thrown at the windows. I don't know what made the driver do it, but he stopped the coach and jumped out of the door and ran after the group of Hibs fans who had thrown the stones. We just looked at each other and after a few minutes the driver returned to the coach, having been kicked and minus his watch, which was stolen. We ended up having a whip round to give him some money to buy another watch.

The away match at Derby County in November 1973 saw a group of us have trouble from some Derby fans. The coaches were parked on a car park a short walk away from the ground. I remember walking up the road and across a bridge and eventually we turned onto the road down to the Baseball ground. A group of lads started coming down the street after us singing united and away the Leeds, songs we didn't sing. I said straightaway that these aren't our fans although they were wearing Leeds scarves. All of a sudden all six of us were surrounded, they shouted Derby, attacked the lads with us and then ran off. They didn't touch the girls though. Luckily the lads were not badly hurt and although it was all over in a couple of minutes, it was really frightening. After the match it was a different kettle of fish, as they met their match when the Derby fans were chased off by Leeds fans. Once back on the coaches there were no more problems but a great mob of Derby suddenly appeared and just walked around the perimeter of the coach park.

We hired a car to travel to Stamford Bridge to see Leeds take on Chelsea in a match Leeds won 2-1 with goals from Lorimer and Hankin. Cost £9.21. Met Carole at Arnold G. Wilson and then went to pick the others up at Ian's house. Little Steve hadn't come so we went down to his house to see why and his dad wouldn't let him come, but we persuaded him because we said we would look after him. On the way down we saw three Sheffield Wednesday fans who invited Carole and I to Portsmouth for the weekend but we declined. To get to the flat belonging to Ruth (Carole's sister) and Alison, it took us one and a half hours to get through London. We went down to the ground in the car (not wearing our colours for once) so that we knew the way and got Gadge a seat ticket as well. A few rough necks were hanging around already. I bought some Leeds badges and programmes before we returned to the flat leaving the car there.

We went back to the ground Steve, Carole and I on the tube and Ian and Gadge walking. Got to the ground with no problems and spotted a few lads I knew. Saw Sheena and some Chelsea fans behind us pointed to her and said she's a Leeds fan. In the ground, we were in the seats in the stand to the left of where the away fans normally stood and we met Sally and her mum. I started asking Sally what had happened to her at Derby when she was arrested and she said to shush as her mum didn't know. We bumped into Mick and Steve (club) and met Gary Edwards, Gary Noble and Wack in the bar plus Billy, Roy Schofield and loads of Leeds fans who we knew, including the South Kirkby lot. In the ground all the Leeds fans were separated but when we scored fighting broke out with the standing fans. This woman sat in front of us kept staring at us. I was shaking towards the end of the match and even more so when a massive Chelsea fan came over and said to Graham (club) you outside after the match. We left then and went to the loos and the match had finished.

The Leeds fans had stood up at the end and couldn't get out without getting knacked because they'd to go through the Chelsea fans. We were just walking out of the ground and I'd my hand on Steve's shoulder to keep an eye him and a Chelsea fan went past, hit my hand and grinned at me. My heart jumped and then his mates grabbed him and called him a daft sod. I'd panicked as we got outside the ground when a tin can came hurtling through the air. We got to where the Leeds fans had to come out and the Chelsea fans were all there waiting as the coppers were escorting some Leeds fans out. All the way up to the tube Chelsea fans were everywhere and the queue was massive so it was a good job I said we'd walk back and then saw Ian and Gadge. It was two miles back to the flat and there were Chelsea fans with us all the way back but once we got back to the High Street we saw a few Fulham and one Charlton fan so Steve took the blue and white scarf off that he had been wearing. We pretended we weren't football fans then but all the time thinking we've won you bums. When we got back to the flat we set off home more or less straight away and when we got to Leicester Forest services saw Fallas Three Legs coach was in. Also saw Karen and Cheesie there who said they'd got chased all over.

Even travelling to Valley Parade to see Leeds play Bradford in the West Riding Cup saw trouble. I took my mum to work first then went in the car to pick Ian up in Leeds. Carole had already organised a lift for herself with Roy. I followed Roy to Bradford and parked up a side street and then went to the Supporters Club where some of the Fullerton Park lot were in. Went to queue up at 7.25 pm and got in the OAP and boys' entrance for 80p and when we got in, found us in the seats in the wooden stand where we sat behind Peter Hampton. Leeds fans ran across the pitch into the side where we were and the match was going to be abandoned if they ran on the pitch again, but they were only getting away from the City fans. At half-time I took my Leeds badges off because a black lad (a City fan) came past us who was after Jock. Then I went back to the others and knew there was going to be trouble as there was fighting in the Kop end. About five to nine all the City fans came into the seats where we were and I was shaking like a leaf as they all stood behind us. Leeds scored but we just sat there and didn't dare move or make a noise. At 9.05 pm I said to Carole shall we go? So we said excuse me and got out as City scored, we pretended to cheer and said typical for City to score because we'd left. Got up to the main road and met some City fans who said you see that lass, just as we got there, we don't think they meant us but Carole and I nearly panicked! Sat in the car waiting for Roy to come back and then when Ian arrived he said he'd got chased out of the ground.

With trouble following me around at away matches you found yourself being verbally threatened lots of times by lads. Instances of this being done by opposition female supporters were quite rare although there were "boot birds" (gangs of girls) going to football matches around this time. Apart from Doncaster Rovers, when I got beaten up, I was only ever threatened once; by some girls at Sheffield United on my way back to the railway station. It was still safer for me as a girl to go to away matches than for the lads, because they would always get attacked and have to fight their way out of trouble. That saying, the intimidation we experienced from opposition fans caused no end of problems and stress; just the fact they were near you was enough to set your heart pounding and turn your mouth dry with fear.

London matches

Arsenal away on 12 April 1975 saw a group of us all meet at Doncaster station to get the service train to London. Leeds won the match 2–1 with goals from Clarke and Hunter. There was Kenny and Dave from Rotherham, the Hull lot with Steve, Pete and Violet plus Jonathan and Nicholas from Rawcliffe, as well as me. At King's Cross all the lads left us because we were wearing our scarves and they wanted to be incognito. When we got to the underground there were loads of Arsenal fans there and most just smiled at us but one got abusive and called us slags so we just told him not to call us that. We got to the ground at 11:40, which meant we had quite a wait until the 3pm kick off. We walked round the ground loads of times and then went to the Arsenal Supporters Club where we met Carole and Linda.

We went down to the ground at 1.00 pm singing as we went. When we got in the ground Leeds fans were loosely grouped together and were singing. We kept walking around the clock end where the Leeds fans were congregated amongst the Arsenal fans. We started to get followed by a group of Arsenal fans who started saying things to us and one said to Linda did she want to try him and got something out of his pocket, but we ignored them. But wherever we went they followed us. In the end we stood above the tunnel and were surrounded by Arsenal fans and got called names by some of them. We had been talking to a Leeds fan from Kettering when the name-calling started so we moved away and stood half way down the terrace. I felt very uneasy in the first half as Linda kept mouthing off and I was sure that someone was going to gob her. Leeds scored just before half time and Arsenal fans tried to cause trouble. We managed to get away from there and move to the side terrace and stood with Derek and Maurice.

We left a few minutes before the end of the match as Linda didn't have a ticket (I'm not sure if that was a tube or train ticket) but we wore our scarves back to King's Cross and didn't see any more trouble. Saw Scunny there who called us names too and said it was a 100 per cent certain fact because his sister was one too. We just told him to get his facts right first. As we were waiting for the train to Doncaster we decided to go into the buffet for a cup of tea and had just sat down when Dave, Andy and Kenny came in and went and sat round the other side. As we were sat there we saw an Arsenal fan go past the window, then the one who had called us scrubbers in the ground came into the buffet area and walked straight through and out the other side. The next minute about 30 Arsenal fans came in and surrounded us. They swore at the lads, kicked out at Pete and then chucked some cups at us. I ducked and one just missed me. Then they went out as the coppers came in who wanted to chuck our lads out, but we said it was us who had been attacked and our lads hadn't done anything wrong. In the end they let them stay. Was shaking like a leaf after that so we decided we had better go and get the train.

The same year on 6 December saw us back at Highbury with Leeds winning 2–1 with McKenzie getting both Leeds goals. Got to London and a programme seller said come here and let me screw you so I told him to get stuffed. Went in the South Bank and stood with a gang of Leeds fans at the back of the stand. Before the match started we could see the Cockneys congregating, although there wasn't any trouble during the first half. This was because there was no score but I didn't enjoy the match. At half time we went to the loo and a load of Cockneys were in the tunnel below the stand and we thought they were going to follow us. I was shaking like a leaf because I knew they were looking for trouble, as during the first half they were all walking up and down the back behind us and not watching the match.

At the start of the second half the Leeds fans had been singing and then Leeds scored. The next minute we were charged at from both the sides and front by the Cockneys. I tried getting out of the way and suddenly there was a gap in the crowd in front of me, and I was stood there at the front of all the Leeds fans with the Arsenal fans shouting come on you Leeds b*******. I nearly died with fright at that moment but managed to get away to the back ledge and saw Violet, where we went down the back of the stand to the side. I hurt my leg in the process and then we made our way to the side at the left with me limping. Before the end of the match we decided we'd better try and get back to the coaches. Just as we got outside the ground we heard a cheer and knew that Leeds had scored so we tried getting away as quick as possible as we knew there would be trouble. Just as we got to where we turned right for the coaches we saw lots of Arsenal fans coming down the street from the left. I had three scarves on which I couldn't hide but hoped they hadn't seen us but they had. One came towards us and two stood round the corner to the right of us and the rest just came straight at us. We wouldn't have stood a chance so I said to Violet to run so they didn't have a chance to think and managed to get to the coach, but then found that the door was locked and we couldn't get on it. Carole and Linda arrived and they'd had the same problem as us with the lads wanting their scarves and little Gary had picked up a piece of wood with nails in and therefore they left them alone. Gary Noble had got a thick lip from going back to the coaches early. Little Ian started screaming at the Arsenal fans and I thought they were coming for us but he'd just heard that we had won the match. Got onto the coach and then we all went mad singing, stamping and shouting. It's a good job we had an escort by the coppers as I am sure we would have had a window put through on the coach, because when we passed a block of flats, loads of Arsenal fans came running out of them so of course I panicked when I saw them.

We travelled to West Ham on a Monday night on 23 February 1976. The match was a 1–1 draw and McKenzie scored for Leeds. Got the 11.00 am train from Snaith to Leeds and went on the Supporters Club bus with Gary, Ian and Karen as well. When we got to the ground we went down the main street on the coach and stopped outside the ground when about 20 West Ham fans came running up as they had been following the coach from the entrance to the tube station. As the coach went round the corner they followed us and stood waiting for us to get off the coach. We walked up to the ground with them following us and heard them say there's some lasses so we dived into their Supporters Club quickly. The others went for programmes and John got mine for me and Ian got kicked up the backside. Carole said they came up to them and said you Leeds slag bags and said what they were fit for. They terrified us. When we went into the ground we all hid our scarves, which was a good job because there were gangs of them all up the road. Gary said one lad said that's the lass who went into the Supporters Club and about ten turned to follow me. I nearly died when he told me that later on. We stood next to the tunnel down the side of the pitch and I controlled myself and let Carole and long-haired Karen do the mouthing. At half-time Karen, Violet and I went to go to the loos and ended up going the wrong way. Some lads said they're Leeds fans and some lads who were sat on the barriers said here are three Yorkshire birds, but they said it nicely and didn't call us names. After we'd scored we heard people running and thought they were coming for us and panicked. After the match we all walked out with no scarves on and when we got to the street where the coaches were parked loads of coppers were guarding the street. When our coach came I said to a copper, "thank you you've saved our lives" and he smiled.

Liverpool and Everton

On 7 February 1976 we made the trip to Liverpool going on the Advance coach. We got picked up in Rawcliffe at 9.25 am but by the time we arrived in Doncaster at 10.00 am we had to call at a garage to see to the coach. We got as far as Everton's ground when the coach conked out and we had to walk all the way down Priory Road. When we got as far as the car park we saw the Hull coach had just arrived. We saw a gang of lads waiting at the car park entrance and saw they were Liverpool fans. We managed to get to the ground okay and saw Mick from Selby who wanted us to queue jump but we didn't. A few Liverpool fans were walking up and down the road next to the queue. At 12.30 pm the gates opened and we went straight into the ground. Someone said some Leeds fans had just been done and had seen one running by with blood streaming down his face.

We went and stood with the Leeds fans at 2.00 pm. Loads of glass/bottles and knives were flying round at the back over the wall. Pete Underwood got on to the barrier and some coppers dragged him off and hit him in the face. They didn't touch the Liverpool fans though and they were all swearing with the coppers stood next to them. The Wallies lot came to where we were stood, Geoff who was drunk, Linda, Karen, Ian, Gary, Kev and Bob. Pete got a Liverpool fan in the loo and nicked his scarf and Bob said they had been chasing them. Kev got hit in the mouth when he got off the coach and as he ran past a fella nicked his scarf. Leeds fans were great and outsung the Kop as usual.

Chapter Fifteen – Trouble at Away matches

At the end of the match I hid my scarves as I didn't know where my coach was going to be. Carole hid hers but Violet wore three scarves back to the coach. As we were coming out of the ground two kids nudged Violet and started eyeing her up. As we were going into the car park Gary Noble, Scunny and the Kettering lot went running past us. As we got to the end of the car park we saw loads of scousers hanging around but luckily two coppers on horses were there. I was walking slightly ahead of the others and two lasses tried to trip Violet up and two kids tried to swipe her scarves. They surrounded Violet and were walking behind us and Violet wouldn't shut up and kept shouting me. Carole said they wanted her scarf. Violet was worried about me getting to my coach before she found hers but I said she wouldn't. I told her not to say anything to me when I had to carry on past their coach so the scousers didn't go after me. So what did she do but say she would see me next week and Pete Underwood said he would see me at Celtic. I got to the end of the coaches and loads of scousers were around and I walked through them, then crossed the road and got around the corner and found no coach there. I was just going to go and find the first Leeds coach I could and jump on it because I wasn't going to stay round there with all the scousers, when I heard someone shout my name and it was the driver of our coach. They had changed coaches so it was no wonder I didn't see it. Got on the coach and loads of scousers were going past but I didn't see any trouble. I had my five programmes (I had orders to get them for people not going to the match) nicked out of my pocket in the ground. On the way home we got stuck in traffic queues going 20 miles per hour because of fog and two Ipswich coaches kept up with us and when I looked round once, an Ipswich fan had taken his trousers down and stuck his bare bum up at the Leeds fans. What a saddo! We lost the match 2–0 but Leeds played well enough and should have earned a draw. Keegan handled the ball twice, and he nearly scored once and did score after the second handball. Same old jammy Liverpool. Linda said a lad from their coach got a knife in his head and there was blood everywhere but he was still alive when they got back to Leeds thank goodness.

Saturday 2 April 1977 saw Leeds travel to Anfield to play Liverpool in an 11.30 am kick off, because the Grand National was being run that afternoon. We stopped at the services and saw a lad I knew and we ended up following him into Liverpool. We didn't realise that the M62 into Liverpool was finished and we should have come off at the roundabout before, so we got lost following the lad and he asked for directions three times. Eventually we came out on Walton Breck Road behind the Kop. I turned the car around and these lads were eyeing us up because we had Leeds scarves on, before making our way down the side of the ground and got round to the car park where we parked up. The three lads went off and Carole and I went up to the ground.

We walked up the back of the Anfield Road end and then went back to queue up where we saw the Fullerton Park supporters coming, so we went to talk to Margaret, Sharon and June. We stood on the opposite side of the road to the turnstiles and then went to queue up just as loads of scousers started arriving, loads of gangs of young kids. One said I hate man utd too. Sharon came over to join me; I think she's quite nervous like me. Sue covered her scarf with her cardigan because she said at Wolves someone tried to swipe her scarf and she had burn marks all around her neck. Carole, Margaret and the others came over to queue with us and then all of a sudden we heard a shout and a load of Leeds fans came running over to join the queue with a load of scousers after them. It was the special lot including Gadge and Cockney, and then I saw Vince and Paul too. They started taunting the scousers on the other side of the road then. There were no coppers around at that time and I thought if they attacked us we'd had it, because there were loads of scousers hanging around. They should have opened the gates at 9.45 am but they didn't open them until after 10.00 am. Got into the ground and then stood at a barrier and saw that there were loads of scousers in our side of the Anfield Road end.

We stood with Gary Noble, the Wrexham and Shrewsbury lot and went mad when Liverpool scored from a penalty because Leeds had outplayed them and we'd out sung the scousers as usual. In the second half all of a sudden all the Leeds fans came rushing over to us and we got crushed. I wondered what the hell they were running for and it turned out the scousers were brandishing knives. Liverpool scored again and the Leeds lot charged at them so we moved away from there.

About ten minutes to go the majority of Leeds fans decided to go but then they all stopped because the scousers were all waiting outside. Jock was watching from the car park after the match and he said Leeds got chased all over and loads got knacked. Karen got smacked in the stomach by some lads and a scouser stuck up for her and told them to leave her alone but she was terrified. Alan Kaye got done again and two of Cheesie's mates got left in Liverpool. I went and stood with Carole as Janet, who had been stood with her had already gone. A copper went running up to the back of the stand and he was talking into his walkie-talkie radio and I knew there was trouble outside. I said to Carole watch your scarves and I'd still got a scarf round my neck. As we were going out of the ground these two kids shouted over here so Carole shoved her scarves up her jumper. Then the kids said "see those two lasses with Scotland shirts on, they had Leeds scarves on when they went into the ground."

We could see a few kids eyeing people up and I wasn't sure whether they'd spotted our scarves so zipped my cardigan up and we got to the car park with no bother and there were only a few hanging around. Jock was already waiting by the car. We got in the car and locked the doors and had to wait ages for Ian to come and Sean had come back with him. I drove out of the car park and quite a few scousers were still coming back after going for the coaches. We came up to the back of the Kop and my scarf was showing. We ended up not being able to turn right and we got as far as Scotland Road so we carried on to Lime Street Station and dropped Sean off to catch the train.

We were going up to see the Grand National, which was being run that afternoon and eventually parked up for 50p. We got out and walked to Aintree and found it was £3 a piece to get in so we set off to find the main entrance and passed some scousers who just looked at Carole and I and put their fists up to Jock and Ian. We turned the corner and saw a lot of scousers and they turned round so we did an about turn and started to go back to the car. Half way down a kid ran past with a Leeds scarf on and I said, "Have you been swiping scarves?" and he said, "No we're Leeds fans". I said, "oh yes," as they'd such scouse accents. About six kids surrounded us and one came up and said, "Are you a Leeds tart then? I said, "I wasn't" and the first kid with the Leeds scarf said, "No she isn't she's alright" and the other kid said "Well she's got a nice bum anyway." We went back to the car and I said to the others shall we dump the scarves and go to the main entrance or shall we go and we chose the latter. I ended up getting very drunk later that night and kept falling all over the place and then felt so ill I thought I'd collapse. I could never take drinking alcohol!! Plus it didn't do me any good because I always ended up being ill and feeling sorry for myself. They all thought it was very funny watching me. I lost my Leeds earring but eventually found it the next day when retracing my steps.

The match at Everton on 20 March 1976 was a 3–1 win for Leeds with goals from Bremner, Jordan and Harris. An extra ten Leeds fans got on our coach when we stopped at the traffic lights. We got to Everton and all the Leeds lads were wearing blue and white scarves. We went in the seats and had to go round the back of the Stanley Park end to get to them and there were loads of Everton fans there. Saw Snowy and Les in the stand below being followed by a group of kids. At Everton the kids were sent to find out who the Leeds fans were and when they were told to f*** off they then went and got the older lads who then attacked the Leeds fans.

I was talking to the lads from Kettering before the match. At the end of the match we decided to hide our scarves and as we got out one lad asked Carole what was the score lass. She ignored him as that's how they find out what accent you've got. At Villa they ask you the time. Saw these lads try to nick a scarf off a Leeds lass but they didn't succeed. Got back to the coach without any trouble and the lads were calling me chicken because I'd hidden my scarves but I didn't give a damn. Once again the coach got bricked and had windows put through. Luckily none of us were cut by the broken glass but it was freezing on the coach with some windows missing. Normally Everton and Liverpool fans waited until the police escort left us just as we got to the park and then the windows of the coach would come through. You just saw a group running towards the coach and you ducked. Leeds fans didn't even do anything to antagonise them. Got back to Leeds and went to the Gemini. I went for the 8.10 pm train and whilst waiting in the station saw little Scotty and his mate. Scotty had been hit and they were chased over Stanley Park and his mate went at the Everton fans with a knife. It was the Everton fans that got arrested not them.

Saturday 6 November 1976 was another trip to Goodison Park to play Everton. When we got to Liverpool near Priory Road, we saw a load of Leeds fans going down the road towards the Street End and all cheered when we saw them. I had two Leeds scarves and a Rangers scarf on, Karen had her yellow shirt and dress with patches on and two Leeds scarves and Carole had her hat and scarf on. Gary and the Hunslet lot came to meet the coaches. All the Leeds fans got off the coaches together and came down Priory Road in a police escort chanting and singing with us girls leading them. We got to the corner and Karen told us to wait. As these scousers came round the corner, both Liverpool and Everton fans, they said they're here and the Leeds fans charged at them and they ran like hell. Got to the side where they used to sell programmes and it was shut. I asked a steward where they sold programmes now and he said in the ground. A gang of Everton down that street ran away when they saw our lot. Went behind the Park Lane End and found some programmes being sold there so bought some. We were arguing with Karen because we were on about going in the side and she said to make our minds up, as she didn't want to get done because we were not with the Leeds fans. I asked her if she was regretting coming dressed like that and thought she was scared, so said we'd stop with the Leeds fans, which was probably the right decision. Saw the Leicester lot come in and some of the Leeds fans thought they were Everton but I said they were Leeds fans. Went into the ground and a Liverpool fan came up to us and started talking and said we were looking for trouble when we went to find Linda. Ginna came up to talk to us, passed Hutchy and a Leeds lad from Selby shouted at me as well as some others.

Karen and I went to the bar and were stood talking to the Leicester kids when these Everton fans came and stood at the other side of us. They looked right rough and one had a bandage patch over an eye and it made him look hard. Whilst stood there we could hear running battles above us in the stand. It turned out that Everton fans had run across the pitch from the Street End and got as far as the penalty area and then had run to the sides because the Leeds fans went to the front of the stand. It looks like Karen was right and it's a good job we didn't go in the side after all otherwise we would have been smack in the middle of them. Went back to the stand with Carole and she shouted that Liverpool fans should be at Sunderland. This Liverpool lad came up to us and said that the specials had been cancelled and we saw loads of Liverpool fans there with Rangers scarves on. One of them said that Leeds fans were getting right bad at home. He had been going back to Leeds station not looking for trouble and got caught up in a gang of Leeds and ended up chanting for Leeds with them. There were running battles before the match started and during the match.

At half time Karen and I dived to the loos and as we came out and were going back into the ground saw Cockney Sal so went to the bar with her. We'd seen her stood at the left side of the ground with Hoss, Denis from Hull and some more. As we went to the bar loads of Everton had come to our end to get Leeds fans and they surrounded us. One lad wanted to buy my sleeper (Leeds earring) from me but I said no. Saw the Liverpool fan that we'd been talking to and one lad said ugh to Karen's yellow shirt. Coppers started braying hell out of some Everton fans so we went back in to the ground. The coppers had been getting mostly Leeds fans before and beating them with truncheons. Saw three off our coach taken out by the coppers, some off Pullman were injured and we saw Ginna limping. We stood near the Leicester lads and when Gordon McQueen scored we went mad and then a bit of trouble broke out but not as bad as we expected. At 4.30 pm I said we'd better go and these Leeds lads came out with us who were going to Castleford. I'd told them we were going to wear our scarves. Got out onto Park Lane Road and a copper said get to your coaches quick and f*** off.

We lost the Leeds lads as we went down Priory Road. Saw some more Leeds fans in front of us get jumped by scousers so went down the middle of the road. There were some coppers on the other side of the road and I shouted they're getting some Leeds fans down there so they crossed over. I don't know whether it was those who came out with us or not. These two Everton fans came and walked by me and asked if Leeds played in multi-colours so I said no it was Leeds and Rangers scarves. They wanted to swap scarves or swap a Union Jack but I wouldn't. They said I could say that I had taken the Street End on my own then. Saw some scrapping ahead of us so I opened a Wallie Arnolds door and asked where our coach was and the driver said I'd walked past it four coaches back. Got on the coach and Carole asked where I'd been and I said I'd walked straight past it and a lad had told Carole that I'd done that. As we were sat on the coach I'd never seen as many Everton fans go past the coaches as then. That's the most I've seen go for the coaches, there seemed to be thousands. Saw Scunny go past and Graham and both smiled at me. Ian got on and said four had followed him and he'd asked them how man utd had got on in a scouse accent so they left him alone. Saw a young lad laid out on the path with a copper with him. He was crying his eyes out and he came back on our coach and we saw he'd got a black eye. Also we saw Ginna go past with a copper escorting him. Collar said he'd been in a pub beforehand wearing his Leeds scarf and nearly had a run in with some scousers.

Collar came and sat on the seat with me and Ian. We had just got out of Liverpool and the coach had taken a wrong turning. We were just turning round when a brick came through the window. Everyone was just sat talking to each other and we didn't even see anyone. We stopped further down the road but the drivers wouldn't let the lads off. After a while 11 Everton fans came running down to the coach so the driver drove off. We stopped on the motorway and knocked the glass into the coach. We stopped at the services and we weren't allowed off the coach at first but then we were all let off. Mick blamed me for the window getting smashed, said I was a troublemaker and slashed seats, wrecked coaches, put my feet on seats and fought with lads. He said he was going to write a letter of complaint to Wallie Arnolds and he was going to get me banned from the coaches!! Cheesie agreed with him. It's a good job I knew he was joking.

When the second coach arrived to take us back to Leeds, Mick and some others said they weren't going to let me on. Went and sat next to Carole so Collar came and sat on my knee all the way back to Leeds. Although he embarrassed us you couldn't help but laugh at him and you can't take it in a way that would upset you. I asked how Lawrence his brother was and he'd written a letter in red ink and had said don't like red and white – man utd – shit. We had to laugh. Collar kept telling us about some experiences and troubles at matches and he had us in stitches.

Got to Leeds and when we got on our train there were three lads on, one with a Man City scarf, one with Rangers (Andy a Liverpool fan) and an Everton fan who'd been on the train a few weeks back. He asked if I remembered him. A copper got on the Newcastle train and stuck his head out of the window and asked what I was doing on the train. I told him I was going home. I told him there'd been loads of trouble at Everton. We all stood in the corridor on the train and were talking to the Everton fan all the way to Selby. He said he'd been talking to someone from Hull and he'd said about this lass who went everywhere and the Hull lad told him who I was straight away. The Everton fan said, "They call you Heidi don't they?" He said that there'd been loads of trouble at Everton this year and there'd been none last year. He'd seen them get a Leeds car and smash it up. The Everton lad said he'd been arrested the other week because he'd been watching three lasses get raped in the Street End. Why, when he said he hadn't been doing anything I've no idea! Andy said he'd nearly got done in at Elland Road the other week by a Leeds lad with no scarf on. The Everton lad asked why he didn't see us on the train on a morning and I said I usually went through to Leeds for a weekend. He said his little mate, who I'd seen him with the last time, had been beaten up on the train just before Leeds by lads with blue and white scarves on. Later I watched the match on television and saw Joe's goal. We'd left before he scored the second goal because we thought we'd get done if we stopped till the end. I'm sure we would have as well because Everton fans went mad and came right to where the Leeds fans had been. I wouldn't have fancied our chances. It was a good day out really but loads of our lot got done including Gary's lot on National three. They got back and a load of Everton turned up at National coaches.

Chapter Sixteen

The worst trouble ever!!

Trouble at Newcastle and Middlesbrough

Newcastle away on 21 December 1974 was another match where we ended up being scared stiff. Because we got there early we went into the Magpie pub just outside the ground which looking back at now was a bad idea. It was also a favourite pub of the Newcastle fans. At the time about ten of us went in for a drink and we were all wearing our colours. All the Geordies stared at us in there although at that time didn't do anything apart from one telling me that if Duncan scored I would get f***** after the match. They all made rotten propositions to us. Five Geordies said they'd just nicked a yellow scarf off one of our horrible looking fans. We thought they were the really horrible fans not ours. Some said a Leeds fan had had his head split open and had been stabbed. It wasn't until we tried leaving the pub that they started singing how they f****** hate Leeds and started on us. They waited until the last two Jon and Richard were leaving, we were already outside the pub by this time, and then attacked them. Richard ended up with concussion and we were all split up. Mick Bates had some complimentary tickets for Sue and me but we were so scared we daren't go to the players' entrance to pick them up. This meant that we paid to go in another part of the ground. Some lasses in the ground called us b******* and asked us if we wanted our heads kicking in and we wished we had gone for the tickets as it probably would have been safer than being threatened where we had stood. We managed to get back to the coach in one piece after the match but were so scared. We also couldn't have cared less what the score was and probably were relieved that we lost the match 3–0.

2 March 1977 saw us travel to Newcastle for a Wednesday evening match, which Leeds lost. I left work at lunchtime and was walking from Croda to Snaith when halfway there Derek from Jubbs stopped and gave me a lift into Snaith. I caught the twenty past one train to Leeds. The conductor said he thought I'd given up because he'd not seen me for a long time. Carole met me in the station and we went window-shopping before going down to the bus station for 3.00 pm. She said one City fan last week said I'd got a nice bum and told her to tell me. She said no because I'd get upset and he said, why I think she's smashing.

Got the coach at 3.30 pm and as we got near Washington services we broke down and ended up stuck there until about 6.30 pm. Karen and I walked up the motorway hard shoulder to the services when a Wallies coach passed us so we went to see who was on. Douggie went past in a car with four others and a Pullman coach went past. Saw Gadge at the services and Cheesie, Craig and a few others. As soon as we walked in heard one lad say, "it's Heidi". Wallies pulled out and at the same time around seven Geordie kids came in. Eventually we got to Newcastle about 7.00 pm and when we got off the coaches the coppers took us the back way up in an escort followed by about 500 Geordies. As we were getting programmes the coppers waited for us and I thought Karen was just getting hers and was behind us so we walked slowly but she didn't catch us up and whilst we were queuing we looked for her but there was no sign of her. We stood in the side with a few nice Geordie fellas and we were stood with some who were okay. There were two Geordie lasses behind us who were supporting Leeds too. The Geordies around us heard us say we were going to wear our scarves after the match and they said we should hide them and tried to persuade us not to. I said I was sick of having to hide my scarf and not show who I supported so was determined to wear it.

We didn't have any trouble in the ground and we came out of the ground wearing our scarves but had them tucked in our jackets. As we got out of the ground onto the road I saw this lad spot us who was coming from the Leazes end so I started walking fast to get out of their way. I turned round and saw they were following us, about seven of them. Carole didn't know we were being followed and kept saying "Heidi I can't keep up, why are you going so fast?" and I couldn't tell her because they were right behind us. We decided to go down the back way and the crowd thinned out, when one lad came up beside me and said swap scarves and I told him no. He dropped back and I then heard Carole shriek so I shouted run and with that I was off down the road like a shot and I don't think I've ever run so fast in my life. Got so far down the road and looked back but no one was following me and I couldn't see Carole. I had to have a polo mint as my mouth was so dry and I was nearly sick with fright.

I got to some coppers and went over on my ankle and a copper asked what the matter was, so I told him about what had happened to Carole and said I'd lost her. He said come on I'll take you back to look for her and went back to the crossroads which I'd run across but hadn't bothered to see if anything was coming or not. Went back round the front way to the cattle market but still couldn't see Carole. Passed a few gangs of Geordies but nobody said anything and I still had my scarf on. The copper said, "Don't stand still because the last time I did I got bricked three times." Got back to the cattle market and I saw Carole and said to the copper she had got back and thanked him and he said that's okay. I went up to Carole and asked her what had happened when she shrieked. She said they came round her, jostled her and tried tripping her up and grabbing her scarf. They asked her what the time was, where she was going, to swap scarves, then give them her scarf and then said if she didn't give them her scarf they'd knife her and one lad got a knife out. She said she'd run when I said but at the crossroads she stopped as a car was coming whilst I carried on. She then grabbed a big Newcastle fella and he took her back to the coaches. Karen had got chased by about 20 lads and she'd been fuming because she'd had to go in the ground on her own, and thought we'd left her on purpose. She'd been terrified going up even with the escort, but had said that Newcastle didn't bother her. Last year we'd won and had no trouble and this year we lost and had all that trouble. Saw Scotty and he said now then blondie.

We got quarter of an hour out of Newcastle and broke down again (10.25 pm) and had to wait until 1.00 am for another coach from Leeds and we went to sleep whilst waiting for it. June made us laugh and she was doing the same as I usually do by putting her foot in it. Got back to Leeds at 2.30 am and Carole and I got off at the Clock Cinema and walked down Gledhow woods.

Got to Caroles at 3.00 am and went to bed for three hours then I got up at 6.00 am to go to work. During the night shock set in and I could feel it building up inside of me and I ended up crying my eyes out at 4.00 am, what a nightmare. I was shattered and Carole stopped off work.

The first match of the season in August 1977 saw Leeds travelling to St James' Park, Newcastle. As we were walking past the Gallowgate end we passed three lads and I recognised one with a black and white scarf on. Carole said there were about six other lads stood there and a couple had black and white scarves on and they said in accents that weren't Geordie them two are the best away supporters we've got. Saw Gordon McQueen outside the players' entrance and we went past pretending we hadn't seen him. Carole looked at him and he was just going to smile and say hello and she shook her head at him to say no. We didn't want the Newcastle fans to know we were Leeds fans so as to avoid a repetition of the trouble we'd had the previous season. Also after our previous troubles there we weren't wearing our colours outside the ground either.

We had gone to the match by car and had met Tony a Newcastle fan there as I had got a Newcastle mirror for him. Tony left us outside the entrance near the Leazes but we were at the wrong side of the ground so we went round to the East Stand seats round the back of the Leazes. Saw the three lads again and the one with the scarf on grinned this time. Saw five Leeds lads with scarves on in the Gallowgate getting followed by about 30 Geordies, a lot of them skinheads with boots on and saw three with black and white striped hair as well as shirts. The five lads managed to get away into the side of the stand below us in the confusion when Newcastle scored. When Leeds scored loads of Leeds fans in the seats got up and cheered but when the Geordies started singing you're going to get your heads kicked in I sat down. At 4.00 pm I panicked because I thought they'd all come into the seats to get us but Carole said they weren't allowed in. After the match we walked back to the centre with Tony but missed out the alleys because there were a lot of rough lads still around. Heard afterwards that a load of our lads had got done including Alan Kaye again and a fair-haired lad from Donny. Passed a kid who said where are all the Leeds fans? Saw two kids with some coppers who said it's next to the cattle market and we knew straight away they were Leeds fans. As we left

Newcastle four Wallace Arnold coaches passed us and so we got our Leeds scarves out which we'd left in the car this time and they were all waving to us.

Loads of Leeds coaches passed us when we stopped at the services for petrol. I said, "Where have all those come from?" and a man in a van opposite said, "That's what I'd like to know". They were all Leeds fans and had been in the seats too. Saw some Leeds coaches who pulled into the services sent on their way by the coppers who wouldn't let them stop. We saw some Wallies coaches pulled in further down the A1 and was going to stop but decided against it because I needed to catch the train home. It was a good job we didn't stop otherwise we'd have been smack in the middle of a riot on the A1 between Leeds and Sunderland fans. They had all stopped off at the services at the same time and as there was no love lost between the two sets of supporters, fighting broke out amongst them.

22 February 1975 was an away match at Middlesbrough where again we went on the football special, although this time we had a reception committee. When we got off the train we were followed by a large group of their fans and Flan got arrested. At first we were escorted by the coppers through a shopping centre and then although we tried to keep up with our fans we lost the main group when everyone started running over open ground. Then we got surrounded by some of their fans, who said hello you Leeds slags. I felt like hitting them but we were on our own with no sign of the coppers and it wouldn't have been a good idea anyway, so we bit our tongues. Jonathan and Nicky had gone into Woolworths and tried to pretend they were shopping but got spotted when Jonathan's Leeds scarf tassles started coming out of the bottom of his trouser leg. They managed to get to the match okay though and when we were stood on the corner near the ground, one Middlesbrough fan said that either I was pregnant or a Leeds fan. Knowing my Leeds scarf was wrapped around my waist I knew the answer. Leeds won the match 1–0 with a goal by Clarke. When we arrived back at the station in one piece and were stood with our fans waiting for the train, some Middlesbrough fans said they wanted our scarves and would come and get us. We just laughed at them because we felt brave by then as we were back with all our fans in the relative safety of the station.

The worst ever match at Middlesbrough in my opinion was on Saturday 22 October 1977 in a match that Leeds lost 2–1. The events overshadowed the football once again so the score was irrelevant. I caught the 8.00 am train to Leeds where Carole met me in the station. The toilets on the train were all covered with Boro, we hate man utd and Leeds, Leeds die, Leeds arsonists, I thought great. The coach got to Boro about 1.30 pm. Carole and I didn't take any scarves and walked up to the ground with Mick and Steve. We were waiting by the players' entrance and then decided to go into the ground and went to queue up for the seats. We saw all the Boro getting together on the corner and knew when the Leeds fans were coming because all the Boro stood up and then charged. Leeds fans got escorted to the ground with all the Boro behind them.

We got in the ground and were talking through the fence to the Leeds lot who were standing in the corner. Saw Mick and Colin from Selby, Sheena who said her and her mate had been jumped on by lads outside, Barry Mortimer and Fiona, loads in the seats, the Three Legs lot and South Kirkby lot. We stood at the top of the steps and were able to see what was happening on the street outside the ground, at the back of the stand and saw some Leeds fans getting chased and Boro fans trying to get in the stand. We also saw a Leeds fan getting done in the garden opposite and another fella and his kid get dived on. Leeds fans kicked Boro fans in on the steps in the corner where they were standing. Kept talking to our lot and the fella who supports England and smoked a pipe said he wished there was no trouble; so do we!

We found our seats and then saw the Boro fans getting together at the bottom of the standing area and make their way to the top and then charge the Leeds fans. I was nearly crying. A kid was laid out by the fence, then the Leeds fans charged back and Ian was leading them. They were scrapping like that and the coppers took their time to get there, eventually taking about 70 Boro fans out straight to the other end. There were still about 100-200 Boro fans in fighting all through the match. I was scared stiff especially as we had to get past their end to get back to the coaches. They took some more Boro fans out both the back way and pitch way. I was ready for going home at kick-off and Sharon said she'd go out early to get back to the coach with me.

At half time I was talking to the South Kirkby lads and said, "It's a great place we've come to and I am not coming again". I asked a copper for an escort and he said there'll be plenty of us around following you what more do you want, so I said protection. I thought he was going to arrest me for that. Carole asked how the Boro fans had got in the standing area which was supposed to be for away fans and two said they didn't know, one said paid and one said through a broken window. There wasn't even a window there and we heard later that they had just let them pay in. Carole said so the club was at fault and the copper said I've arrested people for less than that. At 4.15 pm Sharon and I left and saw a lad from Darlington and he said hello and saw the Harehills trying to get out. Just after we'd left, Boro fans charged again and Leeds fans tried getting into the seats to get out of the way and the coppers arrested the Leeds fans. Boro fans were taken away gently but Leeds fans were dragged out by the scruffs of their necks.

Sharon and I got out and saw three lads and recognised them as Leeds fans, then saw two lads with red and white scarves on start to follow us. I said to Sharon if they start are you ready for them and she said yes, but they stopped following us. Saw some lads running up the road and thought they were Leeds fans. We got to the coaches okay and Cheesie and a few lads were stood with the coppers talking about an escort. I went up to them and said, "I'm not coming to this smelly hole again; you can't even support your team." We stood and watched the Leeds fans coming back and loads had come back early. Saw Barry Mortimer and he said, "Heidi you look, well, normal", because I had no scarf on. Saw one lad come with blood all over his face and John from the Three Legs. Gary who went with us to Newcastle and John off our coach got done. Boro fans came from behind us and bricked the coaches as we were standing there so I hid behind one but Pynes coach had a window smashed. Then they came out from behind the houses and bricked us again. Saw everyone arriving, most we knew. When Sheena came she said a Boro lad had stood next to her saying you're a slut aren't you and I'm going to kick hell out of you outside, so she called him a big fat b****** and walked away. Saw Keith from Morecambe then the Halifax lot got off their coach and chased some Boro down the road.

Lads kept telling us what had happened, one of the brummy lads fell down, one said they asked him the time and smacked him one in the mouth, another said that he'd been asked that too. Dave got asked where he came from and he said Redcar, the Boro fan asked him whereabouts and when he said Queen Street he had an argument with a Boro fan who said there wasn't one. I told everyone I wasn't going to Boro again. Passed the Three Legs coach and Gary Noble waved, saw Barry, some others and Dickie from Selby. They started sticking their noses up at our coach so I stuck my fingers up at Barry then said I didn't mean to do that, Barry looked shocked. The coaches had been racing each other and passed the National coach; saw Fiona, Mick from Ossett, Barnsley (England) who all waved. Got to Leeds and went straight to the station and met the special and Ruth came off it, also Phil and his mates (Wrexham) so we had a friendly argument. Steve from Shipley sat with Ruth and myself and then went for his train. Went to phone up home and met Graham Drubery and one of Schulz's mates and spoke to them and had a laugh. Caught the 8.10 pm train home and some Hull City fans were on but they didn't mouth it till I got off the train. Told the people who worked in the cafe in Selby station what had happened at Boro before I caught the 9.00 pm bus home.

Man City and Man Utd

The away match at Maine Road to play Manchester City on 31 August 1974 was also a bad match for trouble. We got beaten 2–1 with Clarke scoring our goal. Although there were a lot of Leeds fans in the seats sat together, all of a sudden these City fans appeared to the right of us. I'm not sure but I think once we had scored this identified where pockets of Leeds fans were. They started infiltrating the seating area and looking for Leeds fans. We had been in their Supporters Club before the match and had worn our colours so we were very worried. We had hidden our colours when it was obvious things were going to kick off and found it was a very intimidating atmosphere especially when you know you support the opposite team to them. Some of our fans were in the opposite corner of the ground on the terraces and it was a match where a lot of our fans took a beating. It wasn't a nice place to go to, especially as there were lots of ginnels down the back of the ground which I thought were very scary. The previous year in October 1973 was another match, which was always going to be a nasty affair for us fans. Although the match ended up with a 1–0 win some friends got attacked and one had his Celtic scarf nicked.

Chapter Sixteen – The worst trouble ever!!

Boxing Day on 26 December 1975 saw us visit Maine Road again. Leeds won the match with a rare goal from Madeley. I went on the Advance coach from Goole and my dad took me to Rawcliffe to catch it. The coach set off at 8.40 am from Rawcliffe and we got to the ground at 11.30 am. Their Supporters Club wasn't open so we had to wait another ten minutes until it was. We'd parked behind the Kippax stand because that is where we always parked and then read in the programme that we weren't allowed to anymore. Mr Gallagher the driver then went to move the coach so no one knew where it was parked anymore.

Went into the ground at twenty past two and Carole, Linda and Karen were just arriving. As we got into the ground I went to the loo, but as everyone was queuing I decided not to wait and as I got back to the others they said some man utd kids had threatened to knack Jonathan. We went in and sat down at the front of the stand and the next thing we saw Leeds fans in the Kippax being chased out. They ran to the bottom of the stand where they were attacked again and then they jumped out and ran over to the seats. The coppers then took out a couple of Leeds fans, which wasn't right. Mick Howdle got a cut head. Leeds fans in the seats started shouting and singing and it sounded fantastic.

Sue and I were scared as usual because we were worried about what was going to happen at the end of the match. We had a talk and she said she had walked through the tunnel with some Man City boot boys with her scarf on. She said a Leeds bird with boots on had said she didn't know how she had the nerve to wear her Leeds scarf. Linda, Carole and Karen said there had been loads of Man City waiting for the coaches and had followed them all the way to the ground. Linda had brought her massive banner with her as well. When we scored we went mad and then Sue and I looked at each other and said "that's it we've had it". Leeds fans started singing Jingle Bells and When the Whites go marching in and it sounded fantastic. We were singing throughout the match and out sung the City fans.

Ten minutes from the end of the match I went to join Mr Gallagher, his wife, Bev and Anne so that I could find my way back to the coach. I had hidden my scarf and I felt safer. Anne and Bev had their scarves on and walked on either side of Bev's dad. At the bottom of the stand steps loads of Man City were waiting and we just walked through them and those waiting outside the ground as well. We walked the back way to the coaches and missed most of the City fans. Saw a Leeds lad who stood near Maggie and Frankie at home matches and spoke to him. We got to some traffic lights where we had to turn right and passed some City fans who said they are only birds. Billy and Teddy, plus Jonathan and Nicholas had joined us by this time. We got to the next set of traffic lights and turned left onto the main road to be confronted by loads of City fans up the road. We then crossed over the road and I slowed down to stay with the Gallaghers because a gang of City were waiting on top of the bridge. Billy started walking straight through them and I was at the side of the road with Jon and Wishy behind me and the City fans just looked at us and left us. They then saw this lad behind Bev and said there's one and all dived towards him and started kicking him. Four coppers heard the noise and came round the corner and started chasing the City fans and the Leeds lad got away but not before they'd hurt him. Passed Linda and the others already on Wallies coaches and waved to them and then the Rangers fan on the Harrogate coach.

The majority of our lot got back to the coach but Sid was missing so two got off to look for him. Eventually Sid got back and the other two were missing. We eventually left at 5.30 pm with everyone on the coach in one piece. There had been a heavy presence of coppers by the coaches but this was sadly missing on the way back to them. One lad had been thrown in front of a car. It was really terrible and Carole, Linda and Karen were terrified as well, as they also had a bad time getting back to the coaches. Carole and the others had been followed all the way to the coaches at City and managed to walk with the coppers so avoided getting attacked, although they saw loads of incidents.

27 December 1975 the second match in two days saw Leeds play Leicester City at home. I caught the Snaith train and a lot of Leeds fans got on at Pontefract. One lad from Ponte said that Leeds fans had been 'murdered' at Man City. Went straight to the Supporters Club where they said it was a waste of time telling us to take our scarves off. Norma told Carole that a Leeds lass had got a broken nose in the ground at Maine Road when a City lad smashed her in the face. A Leeds fella did the same to him and a copper said I'm glad you did that because I'd have done the same. We heard that a Leeds fan had a fractured skull, Paul Tasker from Bradford (we sent a get well card to him).

We then went to the Peacock and were talking to Barry and his mate (from the Pullman coach) and he said he'd been taken to hospital along with 30 others at Man City and one lad had 70 stitches in his head. Two others had been hit with hatchets and the front of one lad's denim jacket was covered in blood. Loads more of our fans got knacked or had a near do.

Got to the South Stand and we saw Fiona and she asked us about Man City too. She said they'd been at Platt Lane police station until ten to seven as a lad off their coach had a fractured skull and he'd nearly died that morning. She also said that the City fans had attacked their coach with knives and bricks and that it had been very bad. We were chatting to others in the Kop about our experiences at Man City. One lad said he had been saved by man utd fans and had to buy them drinks but at least he and his mates were safe. During the Leicester match when we scored we went mad and I couldn't keep my footing along with everyone else on the terrace. Fair-haired John's mate (driver) banged his head on the floor and nearly knocked himself out. At the end of the match we all stood there singing *You'll Never Walk Alone*. It was a great match and I didn't expect Leeds to play great two days running but they were magnificent. Saw little Gary and was talking to him about Man City. Some told him not too politely to go home, in fact said he was a Leeds fan and to get him but luckily he ran and got away. On the train home I spoke to a lad from Selby and he was telling me about his experience at Liverpool. He had been attacked five times from the centre to the station and got thrown through a shop window.

Good Friday on 8 April 1977 and another bad match for us Leeds fans at Maine Road. Carole and I went to pick up the hire car, an R registration Mini. Was talking to Mazza in Leeds and then went to pick up Ian, Jock and Killer who were coming with us. Stopped off at Birch services and I asked a Man City fan the best way to the ground and he said we could follow him. It didn't take us long to get to the ground and we parked behind the Kippax. I had my Rangers scarf on and the three lads had City scarves on. Went straight to the club and met Gary Edwards, Gary Noble and Mel (Gary Edwards's girlfriend), the Supporters Club lot, Richard the City fan Frank knows and stood talking to them. We bought some seat tickets from Margaret for £1.30 each. Richard said we could have stood with them and we'd have been okay. We went into the ground and there were loads of Leeds fans in the seats where we were opposite the Kippax. We could see there was some trouble once again in the Kippax. Karen and Linda went in there and Linda nearly got done. She had to fight some lads and a massive City lass who she hit and made her slip so she got away. Karen wouldn't take her scarves off at first but Linda made her take them off. Saw Alan Kaye going round the pitch with the first aid fellas. He got done both in the Kippax and later going back to the coaches, along with a Leeds woman who also got done.

Just before half-time all these lads came over the wall into the seats where we were, apparently mostly man utd fans (a lot of them were black) and they just sat there staring at all the Leeds fans. This was so intimidating. At half-time we went to the toilets and passed Byron Stevenson, Gwyn Thomas (Leeds players) and the team coach driver and they nodded and said hello. When there was about quarter of an hour to go all the man utd and Man City fans came up the side of us once again. The coppers had tried moving them once but they all stayed there so I took my Leeds scarf off and put my Rangers one back on. Some of the Leeds lads made a move to go out and the man utd and City fans were after them like greased lightening. Ian, Jock and Killer nearly got done but they managed to get away as the City fans went after another Leeds lad. He got cornered down a side street and they kicked him for ages and then left him. One Leeds lad in the ground had said there's Heidi over there and Ian said do you know her and he said no only from the papers. We got back into the Supporters Club and put our Leeds scarves back on and saw Gary Noble who said he had nearly got done as well. We walked past some lads who called us bitches and Carole, Margaret and Sharon got called names. Jock had a glass pulled under his nose by a massive fella. I went and stood with Jock and Richard the City fan who lived near Mazza. He said to me do you know a lass with right blond hair who wears dungarees with patches and had a banner, so I said that was me.

Richard and Jock went with me to go and bring the car round to the club. When we got out of the car all the "mafia" were stood waiting on the corner, all dressed in suits looking smart, but they are one of the worst lot for causing trouble. Also there was a gang with green and yellow hair that go everywhere and always stick together and never run. We got back into the club and when I saw Carole I told her to take her scarf off. She said I am, because they are after us! The lads had been pushing them, calling them names and spitting at them so she cracked one of them and they all said to hit her. I said we'd better go then and got the others as some City fans followed us out to the car. I reckoned that the mafia had looked to see whose car it was because the wing mirror had been moved.

I set off as quick as I could and went straight down to the crossroads instead of turning right the way we'd come, we turned left to go past Princess Road. Whilst we were stuck at the traffic lights we saw the same man utd fans who'd come into the ground next to us, walk past on the other side of the road so we all tried hiding, although I couldn't with driving, the others ducked down behind the seats. I carried on driving straight down to Edge Lane and passed the M63 Stockport, Cheshire road and turned off at the turning after that and came back up the other side of the dual carriageway and got the M63 to Rochdale. We stopped off at Arthur's house and as we all got out of the car with our Leeds scarves on, Brian, his brother Jimmy Greenhoff and Gordon Hill came to the window next door to look. Ian shouted out they wouldn't win at Hillsborough. Got to Caroles and her mum said the *Daily Express* had been round and rung up eight times about Carole's letter she had sent in to them.

Maine Road again on Saturday 12 November 1977 saw Leeds win by 3–2 with goals from Jordan, Graham and Hankin. During the match I came out with some right language because City were fouling Leeds left, right and centre. In the end Carole shouted knack em Leeds and a City fella next to me said, "Is that the way they play?" I said, "You must be joking they're taking a leaf out of City's books and giving as good as they get," he soon shut up.

At half time we went to the loo and Carole was shouting through the door to me saying how they'd fouled Brian Flynn and then this lass shouted, "It's nothing like that gorilla Jordan you're all the same from Yorkshire; thick, you Yorkshire Pudding" and Carole said, "You stupid Lancashire cow". I said, "What's going on?" and told Carole to stop but when I got out the City lass had gone. In the second half it was fantastic, Leeds played great and we scored three times in 21 minutes after we had been one goal down in the first half. I went absolutely mad and then noticed how many Leeds fans there were, loads round us in the main stand, loads in Platt Lane and the Kippax; they were everywhere, Leeds fans singing and shouting. When we scored the third goal the City fans all dived for the entrances. At 4.30 pm some lads came to the side of our seats like last year, we'd no scarves on but Roy and Graham had, so Carole and I went to stand up at the back after City scored their second. At the end of the match we just went out with the crowd and went straight to the club. Alan Kaye got done yet again, he'd told a City fan to f*** off in the ground and when he walked out he went straight into the same ones and got smacked in the face.

At 5.45 pm the coach came round for us and we all went out and got on it. We had no trouble apart from some City fans coming out of the club after us and sticking their fingers up and one pretended to throw something. We got to Princess Road and all the traffic was stopped up to the hill where the Leeds coaches were parked and blue lights were flashing. Got to Urmston and a brick hit the little window above the driver and shattered it.

The following week at Elland Road, I saw Mick and Dave Howdle, Paul, Alan Jackson and then saw Alan Green and he asked if we'd heard about Martin from Bradford. He'd gone to Man City with three other lads and they'd got set on by approx 60 City fans and two of the lads got away, but Tony got kicked in and Martin got razored four times across his face. He said all his cheeks were hanging out and you could see his teeth through the cuts and had part of his nose sliced off. Then the City fans went back and said give us your sheepskin coat or else and ripped his £60 sheepskin off his back. That was horrible news and we really felt for the lads.

13 March 1976 was the visit to Old Trafford and man utd. We lost the match 2–3 with Cherry and Bremner scoring our goals. Sue and I went in the car on Friday night and stayed at the Dawson's house. When we arrived there we went for a ride to the ground so we knew how to get there. We got up at 9.40 am and had just come down for a cup of coffee when we heard a car pull up. It was a taxi and Carole, Linda, Ian and Gary got out. Linda had three Leeds scarves on and said they had decorated the train. When they came out of the station Linda walked up to some hard looking man utd kids and said, "What colours do Leeds play in?" They said "those" and she said, "Just my luck I thought they were Derby Countys what am I going to do?" then they caught the taxi. We all went to the shops and then the other four went down to the

ground on the ten to one bus while Sue and I went down on the ten past one bus. Some lads started following Linda when she got off the bus so she picked some wood up and they ran off. Another one grabbed her by the hair and said did she want her f*****g head kicked in or do you want raping, so she said do you want 'stabbing' and brought the piece of wood out so he took off. They told some other rough ones they were staying at Brian Greenhoff's house.

There were loads of hard man utd fans around the bus stop and Sue and I had put a red rag around our wrists as we had got so scared and knew that if we weren't wearing a scarf at all that we would be a target. Because of this we walked through them all. Got to the ground okay and went in the main stand where we saw John and Nicky. We went down to get a drink from the refreshments bar and this lad came up behind us and said you'll never get away with it. Our hearts missed a beat as we didn't know who the lad was, so weren't sure whether he was a Leeds fan or not. At the end of the match we waited a few minutes and then went to leave and just as we were going down the steps two lads said we weren't man utd fans. We walked across the scoreboard end and then Sue and I were walking back to Urmston along the railway lines and had to walk through loads of their hooligans. One said, "Where are they? They must have impounded them" and another said, "Follow him he's not man utd." Carole said there were some hooligans around them who said, "He's a Leeds fan" and she said, "How do you know?" and he said because his tassles are showing (his scarf was down his leg). They then went and knacked him and got his scarf. Carole also said she'd seen a young Leeds lad of about 18 in the ground crying. Linda said that our picture from the *Daily Express* had first been put up on a dartboard and darts thrown at us and then some decided they fancied us. How true that is I don't know.

When Sue and I were walking away from the ground we heard someone saying Heidi, Heidi, Heidi and I didn't dare turn round at first then realised it was Mick Howdle. We had some man utd fans waving at us from coaches but we ignored them. Then the Leeds coaches passed us and one lad was just going to stick his fingers up at us then they recognised us and waved instead. Alan the Rangers fan waved at us and we thought we would never live it down wearing a red rag around our wrists. When we got back to the Dawsons, we saw Ian and Gary and they had left the ground at ten past four with the rest of the Leeds fans in the scoreboard end. They'd got lost and been chasing man utd fans and stamping on red scarves. On the way home I drove the car and we were all singing.

We went into the Three Legs back in Leeds and the lad behind the bar said I was on his coach ages ago at West Ham then said no Villa in the League Cup when the windows broke and I was a hooligan. Saw two lads from the Hull coach who said a Leeds lass had thrown a brick and bust a window. Saw Maggie and Gill and they went into a pub full of man utd hooligans. They had no scarves on but they kept staring at them and singing about hating Leeds and a lass went up to them and said I'd get out of here if I were you, so they did. We did meet some decent man utd fans so they weren't all pigs. I did get on well with some of them from Selby and Old Goole and I could have a laugh with them.

The following season on 12 March 1977 saw us play man utd again at Old Trafford. Carole met me in the station and we went down to Arnold and Wilson's Garage to pick the hire car up (where Carole's dad worked). Couldn't get the key in the door and we had a right laugh at first. It was an R registration Allegro – Blue. Got to Manchester and I drove down to the ground the back way to familiarise us again with the way to the ground and came back the bus route. There were loads of man utd fans around and it was only 10.00 am.

We went back to the Dawsons and parked the car up there and set off at 11.15 am to walk to the ground. Carole and I went in the Trafford Park Hotel and had a drink then left the others to go to the ground. Some City fans passed in a lorry and one held a knife at his throat. We had a red rag round our wrist. As Carole and I walked up to the ground a van went past us and someone shouted out you man utd b******s then it turned round and as it got next to us they shouted out, they're from f***** Leeds. We were just ready to get our Leeds scarves out from round our waists but were so thankful that they were our fans. Got up to the ground and these pig fans said something to us which, we ignored. We went and queued up for the unreserved seats and saw Frank and Mick were ahead of us then saw Ray, Chris, Esther and Ian. Spotted a few more Leeds fans who we knew. Ian came to talk to us; he was going in the scoreboard standing. All of a sudden we heard some singing and thought it was man utd fans. It was about 30 Leeds fans from the Three Legs all wearing their scarves and waving little Union Jacks and singing we hate man u – the Howdle twins, Graham and that lot. All the man utd fans were shocked to see them and when they ran over to them the coppers intervened and got all the Leeds fans into the ground. There was a new fashion for the man utd birds, skirts, ankle socks and monkey boots.

As we got in the seats we stood there and this lad shouted 'Heidi'. We looked round and these lads all had red and white rags and hats on. I thought they were man utd fans who knew me and then they shouted South Stand so we went to talk to them. Carole then went to see the Leeds fans and they all shouted we love t*ts to her. Saw Sal in the bar in the scoreboard stand below us and shouted down to her. She went daft when she saw the rag I had on my wrist but I don't care, after Newcastle I was so scared that I was going to give myself some protection. These lads from the Three Legs shouted up to me and wanted to borrow the rag and said they'd give it back in the pub. A copper came up and said to me do you know someone down there and I said yes they're my mates and I said I'm a Leeds fan and showed him my scarf.

He smiled then and I said, "I am not antagonising them as we supported the same team". Saw Karen and she waved. Linda smacked a lad for nipping her bum and he was going to hit her back and a copper stopped him. Mac saw a gang following Karen and Linda to the ground. At the end of the match Carole went for a bus and Mick, Jock and I went to walk the back way back to Urmston. We met Ian halfway back and loads of man utd passed us. A Leeds car passed us and they stuck their thumbs up at us. It chucked it down and we were frozen and soaked. We took the red rags off and then saw the Three Legs coach pass and they looked shocked when they saw us. We got to Urmston before the Leeds coaches arrived and we waved our Leeds scarves at them. Wallies and Fallas had a window out. The Scarborough Taps lot went past.

At Elland Road the following week I heard someone say look at the state of you two. We turned round and it was Collar. We got talking about our trip to Old Trafford. He'd gone in the Stretford End with his Celtic scarf on and he said he wanted Leeds to win because there were more Scots in the team. Obviously at that time they weren't aware that he was a Leeds supporter. At half-time he'd sat down and opened his book up but had to shut it straight away because his I hate man u badge was in the middle of it.

Wolverhampton and West Bromwich

Leeds travelled to Wolverhampton Wanderers on 26 April 1975, the game ended in a 1–1 draw with Frank Gray scoring for Leeds. Not many Leeds fans travelled to this match as I think they were only concerned with going to Paris to the European Cup Final. Sue stayed at my house and we got a lift in to Selby station with Jonathan's dad. On the train we met Pete, Violet and some others. At Doncaster station, Scunny joined the train along with some man utd fans and a Sunderland fan. I hit Scunny for calling us names again. We had to change trains at Sheffield and then again at Birmingham. Somehow Chinky and Pete got arrested when we changed trains at Birmingham station. When we arrived at Wolverhampton we went to a pub across the road. The lads wouldn't go in at first because there were five Wolves fans in, we teased them and called them 'cowards' and went in first and the lads followed. Turns out the Wolves fans were quite friendly and we spoke to them about Barcelona and that we had been there. They said Leeds fans were going to get done because they'd got knacked (500 in a tunnel at Leeds), and they would get Leeds next year.

Because we got to the ground very early we went into the Fox pub next to the tunnel leading under the dual carriageway, at the back of the South Bank at Molineux. Then Sue, Violet, Linda and I went for a walk around the ground singing as we went along. We then went back to the Fox and I got fed up just hanging about so went and sat outside the pub. As I was sat there I heard a commotion and saw a gang of Wolves fans coming over the dual carriageway wall. I went into the pub to tell Pete and the rest of them then went back outside the pub. I was just stood watching when I saw five massive Wolves fans come up behind some Leeds fans and jump them. Linda and I got out of the way quickly as the gang raced up as well and joined in, running off with their scarves after kicking them. Linda and I tried to get back to the pub and had to get out of the way of two Wolves fans running back. They said go back home you Leeds b******s, whilst I was in the process of falling over a wall and hurting my knee and hand. We got thrown out of the pub then and told we were asking for trouble hanging around. Unfortunately there was nowhere else to go as the ground was still shut so we had to hang around near the entrance to the South Bank.

Chapter Sixteen – The worst trouble ever!!

We were still stood there when we saw the Wolves fans coming back. They had spotted some Leeds fans coming over the car park on the other side of the dual carriageway and ran across the road after them and chased them. We saw that one of them was Sally from London and as she was running she slipped and fell against a post. The Wolves fans caught up with her and wrapped her around a lamppost; nicked one of her scarves and when they couldn't get the other one started kicking hell out of her. We saw a girl who saved her and was told it was Tina Gulliver who was a Chelsea fan but went to join Wolves fans, as she was too well known at Stamford Bridge. Without Tina's intervention I'm sure Sally would have been kicked unconscious. The Leeds fans on our side couldn't help, as there was a massive drop onto the dual carriageway where we all were and the coppers stopped anyone going anywhere. Sally came across the dual carriageway so we went to help her and the rest of the Leeds fans were all still stood there, when all of a sudden a massive gang of Wolves fans came up from the South Bank behind us and ran at us. We stood there and watched as the rest of the Leeds fans ran to the Fox and Pete started kicking the hell out of a Wolves fan.

The Wolves fans then turned and ran at us again so we ran and got in a cul de sac next to the pub behind the stand and the majority of Wolves fans ran past and missed us. One stopped though and shouted he would rape the first lass he caught. Luckily for us the coppers arrived but then they shoved our fans back and some tried to climb a fence to get out of the way. I was shaking like a leaf at this time because we really thought we had had it. Saw one of our lads with a bruise and bump on his head, his stomach covered in bruises and clutching himself.

Shortly after this the gates opened and we went into the ground. We were okay at first but it didn't take the Wolves fans long to surround us. We saw those who'd caused the trouble outside the pub and Linda was scared they'd get us because she had pointed them out to the coppers and they had seen that. We moved and stood at the front of the stand and were again followed by the Wolves fans that had caused the trouble outside the pub. Linda started talking to a couple and then I wasn't scared anymore because they were alright with us. Two lads from Dudley stayed with us when the rest of them left, coming back to stand with us after half-time. At the end of the match when

Frank Gray scored for Leeds we went mad and they just sort of laughed at us. The match ended in a 1–1 draw. We wore our scarves back to the station and didn't see any more trouble. We met up with the rest of the Leeds fans at Birmingham plus Sunderland and Villa fans who had been on our train going. One Sunderland fan grabbed me so I hit him and told him to keep his hands to himself. There were three coaches of Sunderland fans on the train and they all dived to the doors as we went past and tried grabbing our bums. I got attacked again whilst I was stood talking to one Leeds lad Derek from Grimsby, about Sally getting done. We were talking to some Sunderland fans that were okay but some made some sick comments. I then caught the train to Goole with some 'thick' man utd fans before I got a lift home from Goole with John. Because of all the trouble at Wolverhampton, I wrote a letter to the paper especially with Sally getting beaten up. A small article was printed in the Angry Column of the *Sports Mirror*. I often wrote letters to the papers if I felt strongly about something.

A couple of years later in the FA Cup sixth Round on Saturday 19 March 1977 saw us travel to Molineux again. A kid on our coach said. "It's Heidi, Queen of the coach". Another kid wanted my banner, but there was no chance of that happening. Carole had her 'Power to yer boots Trevor' banner with her and Karen had her United banner too. I had a massive argument about our fans with Carole and Karen and I said they made me sick. I'm not 100 per cent sure why we argued, but assume I was sticking up for our fans but not sure why. Probably it was because of all the 'part timers' coming to the match when you didn't see them from one week to the next. But I look on it as I've said before, that once you are a Leeds fan you are always a Leeds fan. Circumstances change for people and it means that many cannot go all the time, so pick and choose their matches. But one thing that should happen is that the ones that go regularly to all the matches should be at the top of the queue for tickets rather than the ones who pick and choose.

Got to Wolverhampton at 2.00 pm but the coppers kept all the coaches back and took us in together, there was a convoy of around 29 coaches. We arrived at the car park and couldn't get in there because there were so many coaches. We saw the special fans arriving (there were three to five special trains running that day). We parked down a street and then went down to the ground with the Leeds lot, but when we got to the ground they'd disappeared and we heard the Wolves fans arriving, so we went round by the Supporters Club to get my programmes where we met Janet and then saw Chris in the club.

We went to go in the ground and queued down near the boys' entrance. When it was my turn to go in, the turnstile operator looked at my ticket and wasn't going to let me in. I said I'd got it with my tokens from Leeds and Carole and Margaret backed me up and so he let me in. It's maybe getting to the time that I can't get away with going in the boys' entrance anymore now I'm in my twenties! Went to go up the steps, which were choc-a-block with Leeds fans and saw Mark Gallagher. As we got into the ground we saw Gaz Felton and then found out that because there were so many Leeds fans packed in the stand that we couldn't move. In the crush we lost Karen and stood waiting for her. She didn't come so we went back down the steps to try and go up the back way and saw Reeder and he said they'd already got an eye on him. Coppers were stopping people going up to the back and Reeder said, "Which way do we go Heidi?" We went back up into the stand with Janet and managed to find a place to stand. There were loads of Wolves in the South Bank with us. At half-time we pushed our way into the gangway and met Knox and saw a few others who shouted to me. We got up to the back and passed Dale and then saw Karen sat on the rafters at the back of the stand. She asked if I'd seen hers and Carole's banners because someone had swiped them off her when she fell due to the packed crowd. There were loads of Leeds fans sat on the rafters and up the walls of the stand and I saw Gadge up there too. Saw Ski Slope and he asked if I'd seen any of the Shrewsbury lot and I said no. Cheesie came and stood near us and Karen got down.

At the end of the match we saw Mouse, then scrapping started left, right and centre as we went down the back steps. We found we couldn't go out because bricks were flying everywhere, as Wolves fans were bricking us. We could see them scrapping underneath in the bar and saw one lad getting dragged by his leg and others fighting down the steps. All of a sudden we got out, once we were at the bottom of the steps we saw all the Leeds fans were waiting and the coppers were telling us all to get out. The lad who we'd met in the station in the morning had a trumpet in his hand and he swung it back and it hit me on my lip. He asked if I was okay which luckily I was. I saw a lass from Halifax and she'd got kicked in by Wolves lads and had been in the first aid room in the first half. She got her revenge by getting some lasses in the loos to show what Leeds fans are made of. When we got out of the ground Karen and I found ourselves in the middle of all the Wolves fans. We could see them on either side of the dual carriageway and at the bottom near the tunnel going underneath the road so we jumped over the fence onto the dual carriageway. A few Leeds were amongst us but mainly Wolves. One Wolves lad went past, winked and said 'tara', then he said he liked Leeds birds best. We ran up to the top and a Wolves kid said 'shit', so I told him where to go. Got to the car park and met Reeder and he said that he had just been bitten by a dog, luckily I wasn't when I nearly tripped over one. Saw Phil Beeton as we went down to the coaches and all the Leeds fans were down there and we walked down with two Leeds lads. Carole went mad when she found out about her banner going missing. As we were talking to Jock and Ian loads of Leeds fans arrived together back at the coaches. Ian said he got smacked in the mouth at half time when Wolves fans charged.

I told Linda that the first Wolves fan I saw was the big fat one who started the trouble two years previously, but that was the most Wolves fans I'd ever known today. Got to Leeds and we were all singing. Sharon, June's mate from the Supporters Club got hit with an iron bar at Wolves and had five stitches in her head. The following home match I was talking to Alan Kaye. They'd got a brick through their car window at Wolves and one lad got cut with glass but the hospital refused to treat him because they came from Leeds.

I suppose what Carole and Karen had said about Leeds fans only turning up for the big matches was probably true. At the home match after the Wolves cup match we pushed our way up to the top of the Kop and found out the crowd was a pathetic 18,700 but these were all true fans. It was so disappointing to see such a small crowd after seeing all the Leeds fans going to Wolves in the cup.

The following season at Wolves a few of us were walking down to the ground. It seemed deserted when Carole, Mick Whiteley and I walked down with our scarves on and as we came to some steps two lads walked up them and said something threatening to Mick. We got to the club, went in and got programmes and saw some of the Hull lot were in and they waved. Saw Tony from Walsall and he was all dressed up in a suit and looked very smart and we told him so. We were talking to him and looked up when Ian and Mick came into the club and just after that some Leeds fans came racing down the ginnel to the club with some Wolves fans after them. Karen and Cheesie had also got in just in time. Steve Akester came and sat with us for a while and said they'd come on the Advance coach because their coach company won't take them anymore, because they'd had a window put through at Arsenal, the first time in two years. We got talking to some lads off our coach. Mick from Selby, Dickie and another lad came in, then just after that some Wolves fans came down the ginnel again and then went, once all the Leeds fans had gone into their supporters club. Saw Timmy Deighton (with his scarf on), Martin Knowles and another fella walk down, who said they'd walked into them and the Wolves fans put their fists up but parted and let them through. Saw Barry Mortimer, John, Jock and another two come but they couldn't get in the club, as it was full. They waved to me and Baz shouted hello when I passed the door, also saw a lad from the Three Legs who said hello.

Went in the seats down the side and some Leeds fans were in singing. Saw Milly and Reeder and they said something so went over to see them. Loads of Leeds fans were coming in to our stand and there were other Leeds fans in the South Bank in the corner (approx 1,000). Allan Clarke came in and sat in front of us, three rows down. Scrapping started in the South Bank and the Leeds fans got surrounded. There were loads of Leeds fans in the seats and they chanted and sang and went mad when Leeds scored. I kept watching the trouble. Saw two Leeds lasses in the South Bank with scarves, shirts and waistcoats with patches on and they became surrounded by Wolves fans but luckily they were okay and left when Wolves scored their second goal. Alan Green had got hit on the head; saw Kaz and then Mick Smith who had been kicked out. The Leeds fans who were left in the ground got an escort back to the coaches.

On 22 October 1975 we travelled to West Bromwich Albion for the Johnny Giles testimonial, which Leeds lost 3–1 with McKenzie scoring for Leeds. Before we set off from Leeds we saw Jimmy Armfield at the ground and he waved to us from his office. We saw the lad with patches on his jacket from Goole way and were stood talking to him. I noticed Joe Jordan in the back of Sheila's café and he smiled at me, I smiled back whilst nearly dropping through the floor and then spoke to Sid Owen and Bob English who asked us if we were going to West Brom. We went on the Supporters Club coach and they wouldn't let Mick Howdle on, but I'm not sure of the reason why. Linda was meeting us at the ground so there was Karen, Carole and myself on the coach and was talking to Barry on the way down.

Before the kick off we walked around the ground waving Karen's 'Good Luck Johnny Giles from Leeds Fans' banner. Met some more Leeds fans in the pub and then Gary Noble and his mates came in. We went in the boys' entrance rather than the adults, as it was cheaper to get in there and went right to the front behind the goal. The first half was okay and Linda and quite a few Leeds fans arrived and we made quite a noise. Barry was in the side at the other end of the ground and he said he could hear us from there. At half-time four lads with Birmingham accents and Leeds scarves came to talk to us, asking where we had parked, I said over there vaguely and then they disappeared. Because we were right at the front Trevor Cherry smiled at us and Terry Yorath laughed at us when we were singing. Also, during the match in the first half when the ball was at the other end of the pitch, we struck up a right conversation with John Osborne their goalie and he was really great. Shortly after the second half had started the Birmingham lads came back with some West Bromwich fans and started shouting for both West Brom and Birmingham and calling us names. One of them was wearing a white cardigan. They wanted our scarves and banners and we got scared but a copper told them to move back. One of them told Jonathan that as soon as the final whistle blew he would be dead on the floor.

Because of this we decided to move to the side of the stand near to where the coppers were and asked if we could go into the side stand but they wouldn't let us. Eventually though they relented and let us move into the seats at the side and a photographer came and took our photos. The group of lads came to the bottom of the stand singing super sluts to us; swines. As soon as the final whistle blew us girls dived into the loos and we could hear the gang waiting for us outside. We eventually came out where the players' entrance was, but still inside the ground. We asked one of our lads who was there if the gang of lads were outside the ground and he said they were on the opposite side of the road. The next thing we knew, the pratt with the white cardy on went past and saw us there and said he wanted to say tara to us. We moved away and one of his mates tried to grab Roy's scarf but he moved and the next thing Morris was kicked in the goolies. We ran for the coppers who said they couldn't arrest anybody without any proof.

We waited for the players to come out and as we were waiting spoke to the driver of the coach. When the team came out we saw Bob English and I asked for a lift because we had been chased. He said, "Well a good looking girl like you can expect to get chased but they still didn't give us a lift!" I said, "Well played" to Billy when he came out. He said, "Hello love, have you got your book signed yet?" and I said "no" (my photo album was down at Elland Road waiting to be signed by the players). Norman said hello and gave us a grin. Mick Bates waved and then nudged Duncan McKenzie and pointed at us and started talking about us then waved to us as the coach left.

Once the coach had gone we set off for the Supporters Club again because our coach wasn't leaving until late when the West Brom gang came out of the pub so I ran back to the main entrance. When I looked back Karen and Linda had been been stopped by the lad with the white cardy on. The next thing I saw one of them on the floor so I banged on the door of the ground and told them to get the coppers. Karen had been knocked to the floor, kicked by one of them and they had tried to nick her scarf. She came crying to us and the next minute they were coming at us with bricks and bottles. So I banged on the door again and shouted at them to let us in. This time they opened the door and let us in and the coppers arrived. One asked if it was the same gang who had been troubling us in the ground and we said yes. He escorted us to the Supporters Club and said he would come back for us at 10.50 pm to get the coach. Later on Barry ran on ahead of us with a stick as the copper hadn't come back by the time we went back to the coach at 10.45 pm but by then the streets were deserted and there were no more incidents. When we stopped off at the services these lads were there and one asked if I supported Leeds. I said, "How did you guess?" as obviously I was still wearing my colours. With that another lad there called me a twat. The first one saw that he had upset me and asked him why he couldn't keep his big trap shut. I was totally sick of lads after tonight.

Chapter Seventeen

Friendlies and Testimonials

7 May 1974 saw 12 of us go up on the train to Middlesbrough for a testimonial for one of their players, Bill Gates. We had to change trains at Darlington both going and coming back. We went in a pub before the match and met some very hostile people up there. To say we hadn't played them before we weren't really expecting that. Although they were hostile I never anticipated any major troubles for Leeds fans if we played them in future. How wrong could I be because whenever we did play them at Ayresome Park, there was always lots of trouble. We went to the players' entrance after the match and knocked on the coach window to Terry Cooper who nodded and smiled at us. Frank Gray was just staring at us all. I eventually got home at 4.00 am.

On 11 February 1976 a group of us made the long trip to Celtic for a friendly. Leeds won the match 3–1 with goals from Eddie Gray, Clarke and McNiven. Caught the 11.00 am train to Leeds and Carole met me in the station. There was Carole, Karen and John, myself, Gary Noble, Dillon, three more lads about our age, plus two young lads and one older fella. Karen and Dillon got drunk. The three lads had to pay full fare when coppers got on the train at Carlisle as they had only bought half fare tickets. We arrived in Glasgow at 4.45 pm and met two more lads in the station from Harrogate. We were singing going down the street and went to catch a bus to the ground in Argyle Street. We got to the ground and had a look in the Tavern pub but Collar and Bob weren't there. We saw Lofty there and all went down to the Supporters Club and found our Supporters Club lot were there on a big coach half full. We'd been told it was full and Carole and I weren't going to be allowed on under any circumstances. I think this was a repercussion for me daring to complain about Pigeon as mentioned in Chapter Two, when we tried to go into the Leeds United Supporters Club on Fullerton Park. Well it didn't stop us going did it!

We went up to the ground at 6.35 pm and went into the Tavern again and met Collar and Bob. Someone wanted to swap scarves with me but I refused at the time, although later I did swap a scarf and was immediately surrounded by Celtic fans. We went into the ground in the Rangers end (away end) and we sang as we went in and someone else wanted a scarf from me. I swapped one for a Celtic scarf with two badges on and someone else came up and gave me a Leeds plaque. We sang brilliantly with Collar leading us and we got surrounded by Celtic fans, mostly kids all wanting to swap scarves, but I wouldn't swap anymore and I refused loads of people. Later some big lads came up and were praying for me to swap scarves but I wouldn't. I was getting pushed further away from the others as I had about 20 kids around me asking if I knew anyone who went to Paris and if I was one of the hooligans. I went to stand with the others and the big lads followed me still wanting my scarves. After a while I was talking to one lad behind us and he asked if I saw any Scottish matches on the telly and I said only Motherwell beating Celtic. Before talking to him I moved away from the first lot of big lads because one kept grabbing my bum and he said how about you and me quitting this crowd. I said no thanks I don't do things like that and he said I didn't know what I was missing. I went to stand next to Collar then, as I felt safe there. We won 3–1 and went mad. The first match I know where you can stand, sing, cheer and wear your scarves without getting your heads kicked in. The only thing that did happen was Carole had her camera stolen. It was in a plastic bag she was carrying and someone made a hole in the bottom of the bag and took the camera.

At the end of the match we all walked back to the station through the roughest part of Glasgow (London Road) as we were escorted by a load of lads that Collar knew. At the station we went onto the platform and noticed Karen was missing and found out that she had lost her train ticket. I went back to the barrier but they wouldn't let her through. Dillon nearly got arrested because he got caught passing his ticket to her and then one lad lent her £5 for another ticket. In our compartment there was John, Carole, two little lads,

Dillon, a lad from Harrogate and a lad with a black coat. We had a right laugh coming back. The fella and two other lads were in another compartment and Sean and his mate in the one after. Sean and Dillon kept having fights and we all kept singing and banging on the compartment walls. We went to the next compartment and said lets have a look at your artistic decorations when the guard went past and we collapsed in hysterics. Someone had put Heidi aggro and Heidi's got big feet on the blind and I was not the guilty party. I was talking to the lad in the black coat and the other lad who were both Rangers fans and he told us he had been taken off the train by the coppers at Carlisle. The lad with the black coat said I had been on the same coach as him going to the Charity Shield at Wembley. He asked where my dungarees were and I said I didn't wear them anymore as I stopped wearing them when I bought my white Leeds jumper at the end of October 1975. When we arrived at Leeds at 4.07 am we started singing as we went into the station. We had to wait three quarters of an hour for a taxi to Caroles where I stayed the night and then caught the 12.15 pm train to Snaith and went to work for the afternoon.

On 14 February 1976 Leeds didn't have a match so Sue and I went to see York City play Carlisle at Bootham Crescent. When we got to York we went to meet Carole at the station where we saw Fred one of the lads from the Three Legs. We walked to the ground and when we turned the corner a cheer went up and all the Leeds lot were there, Dillon, Linda, Steve, Peter Underwood plus another lad from Hull, Mick and little Colin from Selby. We all started singing Leeds songs. A little York fan said all the Leeds fans had come to support York he hoped. I said yes we had so he was happy. Went in the Shipton end and we were singing mostly Leeds songs. Dave Howdle came in with some more Leeds fans and said they'd been chased by some man utd fans. York said they hated man utd as well and when they came in Pete started arguing with one who claimed to have walked down Elland Road with his scarf on. He said it must have been 10.00 pm at night if he did. Heard that one of the lads had written Heidi's big feet rule the world okay, in the lad's toilets.

Was frozen so went to buy some soup at half-time and saw a man utd fan there. After asking why he wasn't at Leicester he made excuses saying he had no ticket; but they didn't need one. I said that's no excuse if you don't have a ticket you still go. He was outnumbered so he took off. The Leeds lot went five minutes from the end but Carole, Sue and I waited until the end. The man utd fans had gone but the Leeds fans had surrounded them and the big mouth had taken his scarf off. We started walking to the railway station and saw the Harrogate lot and the lad (black coat from Wednesday). Saw them chasing the Carlisle fans and one went in front of a car, nearly getting run over in the process of getting away from our fans. Saw Carole off on the train and Sue and I went to catch a bus back to Selby.

Two days later we travelled to Sunderland for Bobby Kerr's testimonial and won 2–1 with goals from McNiven and Clarke. I borrowed my dad's car and went straight from work at 1.30 pm, picked Jonathan up and then went to Selby and picked up Carole, Karen and Ian. Got up to Sunderland at a quarter to five where I parked next to the ground but had taken all my Leeds stickers out of the car first. We went to look for some loos and we asked a Sunderland fan where there were some. He said I suppose I'd better show you, and then he went on about the fact that we would get our scarves pinched and so on. Had to hang around the ground until 6.00 pm because nothing opened till then and we decided to get some seat tickets. Was in the ticket office and noticed two coppers at the car next to where I'd parked ours so I went and asked if it was okay to park there. He said no because the team coach was going to park there. So I moved the car across the road up an alleyway. Was talking to the coppers until 6.00 pm and got on really well with them. They kept telling us about trouble and were quite funny, jokingly saying there was a good hospital up the road.

Went into the Supporters Club (The Black Cats Club) and they asked how old we were and I said 18 without thinking. They said we'd better be because they didn't want to have the coppers in and also they'd let us in as they wanted us to buy them a drink. We met Gary Noble, Gary Edwards and Tony in there. If they'd known we were going to the match we could have all gone up in their van with Gary and me taking it in turn to drive. They'd got seat tickets as well. Leeds played great especially Billy and in the end Sunderland fans were clapping Leeds. We went back into the club after the match and the Supporters Club lot who'd come in cars came in. Was at the bar and saw this kid there with a Rangers scarf on, I was stood talking to him and he said, "I thought you were bringing up a team of all gonners but they played some good football". His mate said to Carole that he thought Leeds were all old crocks but they're not.

Saturday 14 August 1976 York versus Barnsley at Bootham Crescent was another match when Leeds were not playing. Dad gave me a lift into Selby and I just missed the 10.45 am train. The next one wasn't until 13.17 pm so I went for a walk around Selby and met Mick. He was going to the match so stayed with him. Back at the station a man utd fan and two Leeds fans came in who were going as well. On the train one said I could sit on his knee as he liked Leeds fans, especially girls but I declined his offer. As we walked to the ground a copper said I think you've come to the wrong ground, Leeds aren't playing today. Well that didn't matter to me as I would always wear my Leeds things there. As we got to the ground we saw Alan stood with Barnsley (Leeds fan) and went to talk to them as the Barnsley fans stood staring at us. Then Carole and Ian arrived and as she had got her photos from Amsterdam back she showed them to us and there was one of me in the fountain. In the ground a kid tried to look at my Leeds badge and tried to put his hands where he shouldn't so I told him to keep his hands to himself. We stood at the side of the ground with Barnsley and his mates, two Sheff Utd fans and had loads of lads around us, mostly man utd lads. I'd never seen such a scruffy hard looking bunch as the Barnsley fans. One lad had tattooed on his arm, 'if at all my bones don't mend bury me in the Stretford End'. We said we'd help him to do that.

Barnsley is 18, his mate 17 and said Phil from Wrexham was 16. We didn't really watch much of the match as we were talking most of the time, a lot about Amsterdam. It didn't matter really as Leeds weren't playing. They said they'd been window-shopping by looking at the prostitutes and there were some beauties and a lot of Leeds fans had been with them. We were amazed. Near the end of the match these man utd fans came round trying to chat us up and then started on about raping us so I moved away. Saw Barnsley was back so walked back and the lads moved out of the way saying she's back, watch her. Little Barnsley said, "get your hatchet out Heidi" and the Sheff Utd fans said, "Oh you are on first name terms now?"

I said tara to Barnsley and them and walked back to the station. As we got there four lads crossed the road and one was the fair-haired man utd fan who kept telling me to take my scarf off and I kept telling him where to go. On the station the Leeds and Barnsley lads were stood there so went to talk to them. I then went to check the times of the trains and then someone nudged me and another one hit me on the bum. I turned round and three man utd fans were there and they asked me what time my train to Leeds was. I said I didn't come from Leeds and they said, 'what you don't come from Leeds and you've got a scarf, badges and a belt?' As I walked away they said I had a nice bum anyway which followed on from the comments I'd received in the ground. A copper said, 'platform three for you' and I said I wasn't going to Barnsley, so he said 'I wasn't associating with them then'. Another copper said trust him to be talking to the birds. I went back to stand with Barnsley and was talking so much I missed two trains. They went and said they'd probably see me again next week. The next train to Selby wasn't until 6.20 pm so went for a drink with Mick. Got to Selby at 7.30 pm and decided to start walking the six miles home to Carlton.

Don Revie brought his All Stars to play at Oakwell against Barnsley on the 15 March 1977. Because Leeds fans still had an affinity with The Don, loads of Leeds fans travelled there to see them. I borrowed my mum and dad's car and went through to Leeds to pick Carole and Ian up from the station. We had arranged to meet some of the Leeds fans from Barnsley Steve and Paul in the pub before the match. Some man utd fans (there are loads in Barnsley) came in and we had a laugh. They were on about what happened to Leeds fans the previous Saturday (12 March) when we had played them at Old Trafford and another one was telling us how he ran away from Leeds fans. We went to go into the ground and went through the boys' entrance – which cost 30p. Got programmes and went and stood at the side in the Ponte. Some other Leeds fans arrived, Tony, Schulz and loads of other Leeds fans were there chanting against man utd. At half-time we went into the Supporters Club and as soon as we walked in we saw loads of Leeds fans who we knew including a lad who I'd had an argument with about Terry Yorath, who I had 'threatened'. They were all shouting to us. I said to Carole have you ever got the feeling you're being looked at because everyone turned round and stared at us. I was stopped at the door of the club and asked how old I was and I said 21 (for once I was telling the truth). They weren't going to let me in as they thought I was too young. We went and stood with the Leeds lot chanting against man utd fans; it was great singing. We stopped in the pub till 11.15 pm talking about football, trouble and all sorts. I said if we took football out of our conversation we'd have nothing to talk about.

FA Cup Final, Liverpool v man utd Saturday 21 May 1977. I won a free trip as a Leeds United Agent, because I sold bingo cards every week, £25 per head per person for the day out. We were going on two team coaches and we ended up sat on the bed at the back of the first team coach. I travelled with Brenda, June and Lynne. We set off at 10.10 am and stopped at Woodall services to pick a Worksop lad (Dave) up and then stopped at Leicester.

We eventually got to Wembley at 2.30 pm and these man utd fans by their coaches asked who we were and someone shouted Leeds and they shouted 2–1 to us due to them beating us in the semi-final at Hillsborough. There were loads of scousers on the steps with no tickets. We were in C12 with the scousers and it was jam-packed. When we got in these scousers started talking to us when I handed my chewy out. I told them we were Leeds fans and a lad in a red cap-sleeved T-shirt asked if we went to see Leeds all the time and I said every match. At the end of the match when the scousers were singing *You'll Never Walk Alone* it did sound good even though they had lost 2–1. Scousers started fighting man utd fans at the front of the stand as we left. As we were coming away from Wembley saw Graham Stanley and John White. A lot of lads both man utd and Liverpool were staring at us on the coach and giving rude signs and saying stuff to us but nothing nasty for a change. To confuse them even more when we got on the motorway we put a Leeds scarf across the back seat.

As part of Peter Lorimer's testimonial year, a match was arranged for Leeds to play a Scotland X1 on Wednesday 9 November 1977. Eventually got to Leeds at 6.45 pm and went and got a programme, took it back to the car and went to the club. Met Carole, Tommy, Steve, Alan and Ian and saw Linda and Steve too. Went into the ground and quite a few lads I knew kept calling me a traitor but I was supporting both sides because there were players from Leeds in both teams. A little lad from Doncaster came and stood with us then some Leeds fans started chanting for England. Joe Jordan scored for Scotland. I was stood with Ruth and near the end of the match Tommy started fighting with some Leeds lads with England stuff on. He kicked and nutted them and everyone started so I dived into the middle of them all and pulled them apart and stopped them. I took Tommy down to Carole because we heard the Harehills mob were coming in and starting fighting anyone with Scottish stuff on. After the match I went to get my car and it wouldn't start and I had to be pushed off. A group of us then went to Cheryls before Carole, Cheryl, a lad and I went to Nouveau, a nightclub in Leeds and found we had to push the car again.

In Nouveau the Leeds team were in, although Peter Lorimer was just going out as we arrived and he said hello. We were stood there and Gordon McQueen was stood next to us talking to someone and he was pouring a drink out and some splashed on my arm. He made a comment about not recognising us without our Leeds gear on. Then he told the fella we were the Kop Committee. Norman Hunter and Johnny Giles both spoke when they went past us and Terry Yorath looked straight at me, pointed then he said, I" didn't recognise you". Joe looked lovely in a black suit. Kenny Dalglish did as well and after getting his autograph Carole told him that now you've met the famous Leeds fans. As we were going out Jimmy Armfield said goodnight. I dropped everyone off afterwards and set off for home but had to pull off the motorway for a rest. Got home at 7.30 am, had an hour in bed and then went to work.

17 April 1978 saw the third match I'd been to in three days when Leeds played Dundee for Peter Lorimer's Testimonial which Leeds won 3–2 with Lorimer scoring one of the Leeds goals. Cost 50p for the ticket. We had called in at Ibrox on our way to Dundee to see Rangers play a Scottish select team. On the way up to Dundee from Glasgow I looked in my mirror as I was driving and saw Vivien having an epileptic fit in the back of the car. I ended up pulling the car over and Carole went to ask someone for help and by luck we had stopped at a District nurse's house and she came to help us. Luckily Vivien was okay and the fit didn't last long. Got to Dundee at 6.00 pm and parked in front of the supporters coach and went looking for the club but we weren't allowed in. We were stood outside the players' entrance and then I went to move the car. I saw the team arrive and I got back to the others quickly. As we were stood there I noticed Vivien start to have another fit so we got her into the players' entrance and the first aid people came. I couldn't stop crying then, as

this was the second one in a few hours. Saw Arthur Graham, Ray Parsons and Tommy Gemmell. Everyone was concerned and asked what had happened. We had to go to hospital with Vivien so went and got the car and followed the ambulance. They said at the hospital they were keeping her in so Carole and I went back to the ground.

We got in the seats for 50p but we couldn't join the other Leeds fans that had come because a fella wouldn't let us. We had a do with a fella who stuck his fingers up at us when Dundee scored and Carole went mad at him. A steward came up and someone said to throw us out and he said it's only a friendly. We said that we knew that, but we think he ought to tell a few folk here, as we found that there were loads of unfriendly folk in Dundee, especially after those we met in Glasgow were so friendly. We joined the Fullerton Park branch at the end of the match and had to follow them to the club, because all the Leeds fans who had travelled to the match had been invited there by the team. They weren't going to let us in at first though when we got to the club. Saw the team had arrived and Frank Gray was looking at us. Eddie and Peter waved then they all said hello as they went past. Eventually we got into the club and after the team had eaten we went to see them and they all asked how Vivien was. Arthur Graham, Ray Hankin, Peter Lorimer, Eddie Gray, Frank Gray, Tommy Gemmill, Paul Hart, Connolly (I said I didn't know him and he pretended to be shocked) and Geoff Salmons. Roy Parsons said he was glad Vivien had been kept in because we couldn't have coped if she kept fitting. They were all concerned about me driving back and being the only driver. Paul and Geoff said watch yourself love and I was talking to them and they were great. We left at midnight and pipped at Eddie and Frank and they waved. I gave Simon from Kettering a lift back to Leeds. I was shattered and kept needing to pull over in laybys for a sleep. Eventually got back to Leeds at twenty past twelve the following day so it took me over 12 hours to drive back from Dundee. Stayed at Caroles for a while and then went home. Got there at 2.20 pm and went to sleep.

Left: Carole and Karen with the banner Carole made Heidi for Christmas outside the Three Legs. Right: Ian and Jock at Wembley Scotland v England – on the pitch Ian with his England scarf on.

Left: Muttley, Phil, Cheryl and Carole at Wembley, Scotland v England. Right: Leeds fans at Wrexham for Wales v Scotland – Steve, Milly, Steve, Reeder, Douggie, Dave, Linda and Carole.

Left: Rangers v Hearts cup final at Hampden Park 1 May 1976 on the coach on way home Big Jock, Alan, Chinky and Scunny

Below: Celtic 11th February 1976 – Leeds fans setting off from Leeds station Jonathan, Karen, Gary Noble and Dillon

Chapter Eighteen

Scotland and Rangers/Celtic

Because a large number of Leeds United players were Scottish and played for the national team, it was only fitting that we started following Scotland. Billy Bremner was and still is my hero, Eddie Gray, Frank Gray, Gordon McQueen, Joe Jordan, Peter Lorimer and David Harvey meant it was natural that we followed them away from Leeds. Leeds United would always come first though.

18 May 1974 saw Carole, Sue, Margaret and I travel up to Scotland by train to see Billy and the boys take on England at Hampden Park. We found it quite funny when we were in a pub before the match. We were wearing our Leeds scarves and said we had come to see Billy and the boys. We were asked how old we were by some Scottish lads who started guessing how old we were, starting at 16, 15 then 14 and then said we weren't old enough to be there! It was a compliment really. There were very few women to be seen at the match but lots of drunken Scotsmen. We also had the privilege of Don Revie waving to Sue and I twice and Joe Jordan signed our Scotland flags. Whilst in the ground I was approached by a Scotland fan who had recognised me from the Hibernian match earlier in the season when Leeds had played there and said he had been talking to me at half-time. It's a small world really but out of 125,000 people I found someone who knew me!

The season was at an end but was to culminate with me winning a trip to the World Cup in Frankfurt in 1974. I sold Leeds United bingo cards and one was a winner, which meant that the person who I sold it to won a free trip as well as me. Initially the trip was to be to the Yugoslavia match but then this got cancelled as there were not enough people going to it. Instead it was changed to the Scotland versus Brazil match in Frankfurt where I flew out to the match from Luton. I wore my Leeds things as normal and kept getting asked if I had come to see Billy and the boys, which I agreed with. I went to the players' entrance but couldn't get anywhere near it as it was cordoned off but the look on Joe Jordan's face from a distance when he saw me there was priceless. The match was a 0–0 draw but Billy just missed scoring when the ball crept past the outside upright of the goalpost. A fan wanted a kiss but I managed to get out of it and he kissed my hand instead.

A group of Leeds fans including myself travelled to Wales versus Scotland at Wrexham, Racecourse Ground on Saturday 28 May 1977. We had hired a Dormobile, a type of camper van that had room to seat quite a few people, for the week of International matches. The Friday night prior to this Carole, Margaret and Ian came through to watch me play football. I was playing for Croda Canaries in a charity match against Goole dockers/nurses to raise money for charity. I had managed to borrow a Leeds United team kit for us all to wear through John in the Pools Office and made sure I was wearing number four for Billy. I can remember someone shouting out stop that Billy Bremner when I was running down the wing.

Afterwards we went back through to Leeds, stopped for a cup of tea at Ians before dropping Margaret off and going to Caroles. First I drove to Barnsley to pick Reeder, Milly and Steve up then back to Leeds for Steve, Linda, Douggie and Dave. We carried on to Wrexham and found the Acton pub okay, where we had arranged to meet the Wrexham lads. Got into the pub and saw Phil, Tony, Muttley (Tony and Steve, Wrexham lads), Brian and Kev arrived too, some Leeds lads from Halifax and some Scottish lads were there. Phil then went with me to park the van at his house.

At the ground, we got programmes and saw Denis Law and got him to sign the programmes. We thought it was all ticket and I asked a copper and he said no so we went in the boys' entrance for 50p. Stood down at the front of the stand and had only been stood there a bit and a lad asked me to name my price for my banner. I refused to sell it and he said I was brave to say that. Another lad came down and said, "Do you go in the Gelderd End every week and did you go to Barcelona and Paris?" to which I replied "yes" to both questions and he said that he'd seen me, although he hadn't seen my banner at Elland Road. There were loads like us Yorkshire Scots there supporting

Scotland. The match wasn't too good but the atmosphere was great. These Scottish lads said see the Yorkshire lassie she'll last until half-time and that's it and said something about a bottle. Loads of Scots were coming up to look at my banner and they thought it was great. We arranged to meet some of them in the Beechwood pub at Hampden Park, Glasgow next week. One of Joe's mates from Scotland came up and he said he'd see us later. At the end of the match Joe from Scotland came up and hugged us and some more Scots came looking at my banner. Tony Reeves, Phil, Linda, Steve, Carole and I then went back to Phil's house. This Scottish fella stopped me and said, "Let me have a look at your flag, Yorkshire what a great place to come from."

We had a lovely tea and Mr and Mrs Nicholls (Phil's parents) were really nice. We got changed and then Mrs Nicholls drove us lasses into town and we went into the pub where we were all meeting. These Scottish lads started talking to us and one said Yorkshire is England and I said it isn't we're independent. Dave was already drunk. We had a couple of drinks and then went to another pub and I had another three drinks there. Went to the Fusiliers and it was full of Scots. I'd got my Leeds scarf with me and one lad wanted it and I said no but he swiped my scarf and I chased him to get it back and banged my arm. I ended up with a massive bruise on my arm, but luckily Muttley got it back for me. In the end we stayed in the Tavern until we all got chucked out at closing time. I'd certainly had enough to drink by then anyway and was sick as usual. Half of us stayed the night at Phil's house and in the morning had breakfast then went to pick the others up. Everyone got dropped off respectively in Leeds, Harrogate and Barnsley.

The second of the International matches took place at Hampden Park on Wednesday 1 June 1977 – Scotland versus Northern Ireland. After picking Cheryl and Carole up in Leeds we went via Skipton, Settle, Kendal, Penrith, Carlisle and found our way up and into Glasgow okay at 5.00 pm. We wanted to go shopping and the shops shut at 5.30 pm but managed to get to the shop at 5.15 pm and bought shirts. On our way to Lewis's for a flag we passed a lad with a Leeds shirt on. We couldn't get one there so went to a small shop underneath the railway bridge which was just shutting but they let us in. I got two charms (St Andrews and Rampant Lion for 75p each) a Rampant Lion flag £10.50, and a Scotland badge and I managed to spend £17 in 15 minutes. We went to the ground and parked and then went to the Beechwood where we met Joe in the bar. A lot of fans stopped me and asked to see my banner. We went to go in the ground and at the players' entrance saw Gordon McQueen so we shouted hello Gordon. He looked up and said hello there how are you. We said okay thanks, is Jimmy Armfield here and he said yes somewhere around. All these kids were looking at us gob smacked because he was talking to us and asked us if we knew him and if we knew all the Leeds players.

They were all looking at my banner and we were talking to a few going into the ground about Rangers. All the coppers were queued up and I said is it okay to go in here and they said yes but you can get in cheaper down there in the boys' entrance so we got in for 40p. We stood in the middle of the stand and straight away a lad came up and asked if we'd come up from Leeds because he'd come up from Bradford. He was called George MacAndrew and we gave him a lift back to Leeds with us. We got on great with all the kids around us because they couldn't get over us being Yorkshire Scots. We confused them and had a right laugh. Some were Leeds supporters and one had LUFC tattooed on his arm. When we scored we all went mad and got hugged left right and centre but nearly choked with the dust from the terracing. At half-time some lads shouted what has Yorkshire to do with it and some others shouted lets have a look at your banner, we're from Leeds too. I had my best Leeds scarf on too which made a lot of kids comment on Leeds United. We went back to the Beechwood after the match and a lad tried to swipe my banner but I managed to keep hold of it and George carried it to the pub for me. We had to travel back that night as Carole had to go to work in the morning so after a rest we set off at 12.40 am.

The last of the International matches was England versus Scotland at Wembley on Saturday 4 June 1977. We travelled down to Wembley in the Dormobile, which was full of Leeds fans and found our way to Wembley okay. As Cheryl, Carole and I came out of the car park these lads said slags to two lasses going across the road and one turned to us and said I didn't mean you girls. As we were walking up to Wembley, we passed two lads who said they were at Wrexham, meaning us. We walked down Wembley Way to go and get some programmes and started to get a bit scared because of all the Scottish lads being drunk. One lad asked what the game was with my banner and I thought he was going to get nasty but he shouted his mate to come and talk to us, but we left as we were being stared at from all directions.

We then spotted Phil and Muttley so they came with us and then saw George and he came with us too. We told George that if anyone got nasty he had to look after us. As we were going down Wembley Way we bumped into Schulz and his mate and they said we knew we'd see you here. As we were walking up to G entrance a Scot grabbed my bum and I screamed and Muttley thought it was funny and kept saying so. Went into the ground and saw Linda, Steve, Jock and Karen stood at the front so joined them. When Karen and I went for a drink we kept getting grabbed and shouted at. The atmosphere was fantastic and Ian wasn't very pleased and got his England scarf out again. At the end of the match all the Scots dived onto the pitch and as the majority had got over the wall, Jock, Ian and I climbed over onto the pitch. I waved my flag which apparently was on the television on ATV on Sunday at 5.40 pm which I missed but Carole saw me. I took some photos and Ian had his England scarf on – the only one amongst all the Scots. The crossbar had been snapped in two. As we got back to the terraces and were going out a lad said here you are and gave me some of the turf and said it was from the penalty spot.

As we were walking out to where we were meeting the others a lad asked who I had come with so I told him I was here with my mates. He said lads or lasses and when I said lasses he grabbed my arm and said good, you can come with me to Trafalgar Square and another lad tried dragging me off. I struggled to get them off me and once I got away, decided there and then that we would be better off going back to the Dormobile. When we got back a lad realised I was another Leeds supporter as he recognised me, then introduced us to three other Leeds fans. Eventually parked at Stanmore and caught the tube into Trafalgar Square. We went in a pub and one lad shouted out where's your Leeds scarf and said we'd sat in front of them at Man City. Everyone was singing and it was fantastic. Eventually they closed the pub as it had been drunk dry. It was the best night out we'd had, a fantastic time especially singing songs and meeting great people. A good time was had by all.

Wednesday 21 September 1977 Carole, Cheryl, Steve and I travelled up to Hampden Park to see Scotland play Czechoslovakia in a World Cup qualifying round. Karin and Terry picked me up from work and took me into Leeds.

Steve, Carole, Cheryl and I were travelling up in Cheryl's car. After Annan we kept passing loads of Scots and they all kept waving. Had my Leeds bag in the back window and got shouts from loads when we got stuck in traffic jams. Got stuck at 6.30 pm and it was ten to eight before we got to the ground and parked.

We had arranged to meet Joe Muirhead, Carole's friend, but because the traffic had been so bad it meant we were late and missed him. There were no mobile phones in those days to contact each other! We also missed the singing of *Oh Flower of Scotland* before the match started but the atmosphere was fantastic. We found out later that Joe's parents wanted to meet Carole's friends and we could've stopped there the night plus all his mates wanted to meet us too. Stood with some older Rangers fans and they asked if we were Gordon McQueen's fan club and then told everyone that we'd come up all the way from Leeds for the match. Some kids in front of us were staring and saying they've got Leeds scarves. After the match ended we went to see the players and had our photos taken with Alan Rough. As the team coach pulled off saw Gordon, Joe and Arthur were at the back and they were waving in general and then Joe and Gordon saw us and waved and put their thumbs up. Some kids were eyeing our scarves and banners up and we knew they were after nicking them. A lad warned us what they were up to and he told them to f*** off as he said that that was the only language they knew. He saw us away safely afterwards as we met Cheryl back at the car.

Another World Cup match meant we travelled to Anfield on Wednesday 12 October 1977 to see Scotland take on Wales. Went through to Goole first to pick up Brian, Lynne and Jim then to Leeds and picked up Ian, Cheryl, Norma, Carole, Vivien, Sue, Steve, Jock, Alan and Mick. Got to Liverpool and parked up at Stanley Park and saw that loads of Scots were already in. It took me ages to get sorted out and then some scouser kids asked to look after the van so I gave them 10p saying that was all that I had. Went across the car park and some lads by a car said, "That banner's magic, it's beautiful". Passed some more lads and they were surprised that six lasses were at a match! We got names and addresses of some lads who wanted some banners making. They asked if we would help them get into the ground as they didn't have any tickets so we told them that we'd meet them later if we found any on sale.

I needed the loo so I asked a woman whose house overlooked Anfield if I could use her loo and she let me. As we were walking past the Kop this lad said they were in the Tavern at Wrexham and some others said they were at Wrexham. We went to the players' entrance from the Kop side and saw they were selling tickets so I went back and told the lads we'd spoken to earlier and they went to queue and asked us to watch their beer and banner. When they got their tickets they were over the moon and said we were angels and magic. We left them so we could go back to the players' entrance when a group of lads came round the corner. They were ticketless and had missed the tickets on sale. Some of them mentioned they had got a ladder hidden and were going to smash the gates down to get in. I don't think the ladder would have been strong enough to smash the gates down so maybe they thought they could climb over the walls instead? As we were standing near the gates, a lad came up to us and asked me if I remembered him. It was the same lad that saved us from some kids who were after nicking our scarves and banners outside Hampden Park.

As I tried getting into the ground the coppers wouldn't let me take my stick from my flag in and took it off me. As we got into the stand in the ground a load of lads started shouting Leeds at us; they were Leeds fans and had come by car. We saw that there were running battles in the Kop with loads of lads fighting but I don't know why. The turnstiles in the Anfield Road end had been closed earlier as the ground was full, however, we heard that the gates had been smashed in and loads more fans piled in causing it to become overcrowded. At the end of the match the coppers wouldn't let Scotland do a lap of honour when they won the match 2–0 because they were concerned about trouble, as there were so many drunken fans. A fella behind me said, "How did you manage to survive that? I don't know how you did it but congratulations," so I told him I always do survive. Obviously all of the toilets in the ground were out of order, as there were loads of lads having a wee against any available space after the match. I didn't know where to look so just kept my head down and carried on walking. When we got back to the van, the one next to ours had had the back window smashed, broken into and all their money and clothes had been pinched. They had refused to give some money to the scousers to look after their van. I didn't know it until after the match but Norma had also given some money to the lads to look after our van but it had been a small price to pay really, even if I didn't agree with it in principle.

In the seventies there was rivalry between Leeds fans supporting Glasgow Rangers or Celtic as well as Leeds. Chants would go up during the match with some chanting Rangers and another group chanting Celtic. Collar was prominent in supporting Celtic and Big Jock supported Rangers. New Years Eve saw us go into Leeds as we were travelling up to the Rangers versus Celtic match at Ibrox on 1 January 1976. Leeds didn't have a match and we were going up on Jock's coach. Karen met me in the station and said she'd seen Dave Stewart and he'd asked her where she was going. She said what are you doing down here when we're going up there and he said we were supporting the right team. Linda came and then we went straight to the Three Legs.

Later we met Collar and Bob in there and were invited to Bob's New Years Eve party in the Harehills area. Collar was the only Celtic fan allowed to go on Jock's coach as the rest of us were supporting Rangers. I had three gin and bitter lemons in the pub and three vodka and limes at the party and I became very dizzy and couldn't see properly. Karen got drunk and started crying. She was talking and I interrupted her, so we ended up having a bit of an argument. She said that I had to listen to her as she felt I was a threat to her and any relationship she wanted. Personally I couldn't see any problem because I had a very low self-esteem and said if they were as ugly as me they'd realise they'd have a problem. Karen said she knew loads of lads who wanted to go with me and I told her not to be silly. The only thing going for me was that I had a lovely figure, but even then I didn't appreciate the fact at the time as I thought I was fat and was always trying to get thinner! I fell asleep under the table with the effects of the alcohol. We set off walking into town at 5.00 am and got there at 6.15 am and the coach was already there. The Harrogate lads were at the front plus Barry, Scunny, Alan J. and the coach was full. I sat next to Linda and was frozen probably because I had a bad hangover and felt sick.

We got to Glasgow at 12.00 lunchtime. Everyone got souvenirs and then we went to the Supporters Club to find the others had already gone in. We told them we were from Leeds and they said to come in. It was nice seeing a picture of the Queen hung up on the wall. Two lads off the coach said they had seen us in the paper, before we got our tickets for Paris. I went and bought a

Rangers beret and some badges. When we went into the ground everyone was staring at us, probably because we were wearing our Leeds scarves. We started following some more off our coach and then saw a lad with a Leeds scarf on and he came to talk to us before Jock came and joined us. We wished that we knew all the songs, as the atmosphere was amazing. Rangers won the match and when they scored this fella kissed all our hands. At half time a lad next to Linda called his mates over and they started talking to us. We said we came from Yorkshire not England. At the end of the match all the Rangers fans going past our coach saw the Fallas of Leeds name on the side and were waving to us when they saw all the Rangers fans on it.

On the way home I had been asleep most of the way when it started to snow so we stopped at Carlisle instead of Dumfries. We got off the coach and went to the first pub, and then some wanted something to eat so we went to the Kings Head. The lads went upstairs to eat and we went in the pub downstairs. As soon as we walked in a woman asked Karen how old she was. She said 18 (although she was still underage), then they said Linda wasn't 18 even though she was, but somehow we managed to get served and were stared at by some lads. The rest of the Leeds fans came in and we started singing Leeds songs and these Carlisle lads asked if I was Collar's girlfriend because he'd said he had spent New Years Eve picking me up from underneath tables. I said no. Back on the coach Hutchy from Ripon came to sit with us for the rest of the way back to Leeds.

On the 1 May 1976 we went to Scotland to see the Rangers versus Hearts Scottish Cup Final at Hampden Park where Rangers won 3–1 with goals from Parlane (2) and MacDonald. Went through to Leeds on the Friday night and stayed at Linda's house in Morley before we caught a taxi at 5.15 am. Went to the bus station and met all the nutters. Mick the Rangers fan who went to QPR, had sprayed Glasgow Rangers FC and LUFC on the walls. On the coach the lads kept passing dirty books around but we wouldn't look. I kept trying to go to sleep and every time Jock went past he would smack my bum.

Got to Hampden Park at 12.15 pm and got some programmes then went straight to the pub. One of the lads asked someone which was the nearest and a fella directed them to the Beechwood. All the Rangers fans kept saying Leeds United, have you come from Leeds? One lad told us we were all mad and we ended up stood talking with him and his mates. One lad swapped a scarf for Sue's hat and the other lad wanted to buy my scarf for £3 but I said I wanted to swap my scarf so did that with his mate. The Rangers end was all ticket so we went in the side but was told after that if we'd put £1 on the turnstile we'd have got in that end. We stood as near to the end as we could where a few off our coach were too, including Mick and the little fair-haired lad. The atmosphere was fantastic and Rangers completed the treble by winning 3–1 (League Cup, Scottish Cup and Premier League). The pigs lost to Southampton at Wembley in the FA Cup final and all the Rangers fans were saying fantastic, f*** Tommy Docherty and man utd. We all went mad and Sue and I were crying tears of joy, as we were so happy. We went out chanting Southampton and all the Rangers fans were asking who'd won and they all went mad when we said Southampton.

When we got back on the coach everyone was going mad shouting Southampton, Leeds and Rangers and we hate man u and the coach was rocking like mad. All the Rangers fans were waving. We stopped in Dumfries from 8.00 pm till 10.00 pm. We went into a pub and then upstairs to some sort of disco where some Rangers fans joined us and I took some photos. I rang Carole up and then she phoned me back and we were going mad about man utd losing as it made our day. I'd just been bought a drink and the bar staff told us to drink up so I had to quickly down one and a half glasses quickly. Was feeling very merry and met up with the others and went down the road singing if you hate man u and all the Rangers fans joined in. Got back to the coach and some of our lot had sprayed Leeds all over. I took some more photos on the coach and then someone nipped my bum and I turned round to hit them and everyone started and I had a right fight with some trying to get them off me. Managed to get back to my seat and one of the Harehills lot sat next to me and wouldn't stop going on about Germans (basically Hitler and the war) and drove me round the twist and when I tried to move he stopped me. I was glad to get to the services.

Had a quick cup of tea and then went back to the coach as I had decided to move nearer the front and got my things. I had just put them on the luggage rack when some of the lads came back and I had to fight them off so said I was going to sit on the front step of the coach to keep out of the way. Two others tried to drag me to the back of the coach but Jock stopped them. Alan from Seacroft said that if they wanted to rape me they would and there would be nothing I could do about it. I said I'd jump off the coach first. Luckily the South Standers stuck up for me and kept me with them and looked after me. They said I was safe sat at the front of the coach with them but if I went to the back of the coach to the Gelderd Enders, I'd get attacked. The normal comments from the lads ensued with offers to show me how to do things, which I declined. At least staying at the front of the coach I managed to get back to Leeds in one piece!

9 October 1976 as Leeds didn't have a match I decided to travel to Villa Park with Vivien to see Rangers play Aston Villa. The match ended up being abandoned on 53 minutes with Villa winning 2–0. On arrival at Leeds station Karen, Ian, Jock and Charlie were waiting for me and I was berated for being three-quarters of an hour late as I had overslept and missed my train. We went to Wallies to get our tickets for Norwich before I went back to the station to meet Vivien to travel to the match. At Sheffield, Dick – a man utd fan from Scunthorpe – got on the train and sat with us. He said he knew Scunny and called him Ayl. At Birmingham station some Rangers fans arrived at the same time as us. As we were getting tickets for Aston station we saw a Leeds fan from Darlington (Kev who'd been on the Rangers coach to the final). He said he thought I'd be there, as he didn't think I'd miss it. Got to Aston and walked up to the ground and there were loads of Rangers fans there. We went into a pub and I rang Karen up, she was in the Three Legs pub in Leeds at the time. Got to the ground and went straight in to the Holte End (Villa's end). This meant all the Villa fans ended up in the open end. Those who did come into the Holte End ended up going out to the other end straight away rather than stay in there. A lad came on the pitch from the open end with a Celtic scarf or flag and came and waved it at the Rangers fans. About ten Rangers fans charged onto the pitch after him and all the Villa fans in the opposite end scattered. We went to the back of the stand and stood there but then some lads came up and one kept putting his hands on me so I moved and Dick said it would get worse than that. We went to look for Vivien's mates and these lads shouted us over for a kiss. Vivien went but I didn't and they ended up nearly eating her. This lad shouted me over for a kiss but I said no chance. I stood with Dick but lost Vivien as she went off with some lads.

At half-time all the Rangers fans were getting drunk and they'd wrecked a refreshment hut and got all the crates of beer out and were smashing bottles. We decided to go down to the front of the stand as things were getting out of hand and all the Rangers fans were staring at us. We got down to the front and I bought a badge then sat on a barrier. I hid my Leeds scarf then, as I knew I would have been targeted for being English although I am from Yorkshire. Then bottles started flying and battles started at the top of the stand so I was glad we'd moved. Started watching the second half and when Villa scored a second goal that was it.

Battles started again, bottles went flying and everyone came racing down the stand to the front. I was shaking like a leaf at this point so decided to get out of it all and climbed over the wall of the stand and went into the seats at the side. A fella helped me up and I grazed my leg. The trouble was terrible with loads of people injured and I was absolutely terrified as I never expected anything like this to happen. Some more Rangers fans who climbed into the seats as well were calling those left in the Holte End f***ing animals and were ashamed to call them Rangers fans and booing them. Everybody got onto the pitch, admittedly a lot to get away from the trouble, but many Rangers fans started running towards the Villa fans and they just scattered. The match was then abandoned at 4.15 pm due to Rangers fans rioting, so I left with Dick to go back to the station. We passed the First Aid room and there were lads on stretchers and I saw a lass covered in blood. As we were walking past the Holte End the gates were still shut and they were trying to knock the gates down to get out. I could hear them running and smashing bottles inside.

Walked down to Aston station and a couple of lads caught up with us, asked if I was the lass from Leeds and they said they had seen me in the station. One asked why I supported Rangers and how many times had I seen them play. They went to Walsall whilst we went to Birmingham and they shouted tara and said we'll see you again sometime. Saw Kev with his man utd and Liverpool friends and went into the buffet. As we were going there saw the Cockney Whites and Hoss and another one came up and grabbed my bum saying I had a lovely bum. Some more scousers came in and one asked if I wanted to sleep at his house that night so I ignored him. I was talking to a little kid and he said something and Kev said I'm a Leeds fan and so is she. We eventually got chucked out of the buffet and then I saw the Cockney Whites come back so I went across to talk to them and the lad grabbed my bum again and I told him to get off. Hoss told him to keep his hands to himself when another lad came up, rested his head on my shoulder and I realised I had seen him earlier in the ground and thought that he looked familiar. They asked if I was going to Norwich and said they'd see me there.

As we got onto the platform we heard these lads talking and said someone had got stabbed. On the train I sat with Dick and two lads from Leeds, Steven and his mate and some Sheff Utd fans got on and we talked to them before they went and sat down elsewhere. As I went to the buffet on the train the Sheff Utd fans said here's the part-timer. Saw Kev there and he said I thought you wasn't getting the same train as us and I said I didn't realise it would be the same one. A Rangers fan grabbed my hand and kissed it and said he was a romantic at heart really. Got a cup of tea and as I was on the way back to my seat Kev said he thought that I would buy him a pint at least and I said that I was full of tricks like that. Had to change trains at Sheffield and had a half hour wait for the train so went into the buffet where I saw Janet Milner from Selby. Went and got on my train and Dick said he'd tell Ayl he'd seen me and ask him what he was playing at sending his troublemakers to the match. He said he'd look out for me at Old Trafford. I sat with Steven and his mate into Leeds and a fella came up and gave me a Rangers pendant.

Back in Leeds I went to the Three Legs and spoke to Gill and Maggie. Saw the two lads who I used to give polos to and said I hadn't seen them for ages. Loads wanted to buy my Rangers scarf from me. Drew wanted my Tammy (Tam O'Shanter or beret as I called it) – for his Scotland shirt but I wouldn't swap. His mate said you're Heidi aren't you. Saw the lad from the Wallies coach at Arsenal who we took prisoner and he came to talk to us. David Reid said he liked my colours; George Boyd came in, and then saw Adda and he asked where I'd been. Sean gave me my badge back that had got nicked by the Harehills lads on our way back from Boro.

Above: Jamie, Michelle and Heidi

Left: Phillip and Danielle, 5 weeks old August 1992 with the League Trophy

In the Peacock Garden, Burnley May 2011 – Heidi, Michelle, Laura, Carole, Ashley, Sue and Paul

Burnley last match of season, May 2011 – Michelle, Laura, Sonya, Danielle, Hannah, Emily, Heidi and Sue

Unveiling of Don Revie Statue, 5 May 2012 – Danielle, Heidi and Emily

Chapter Nineteen

Summing up my dedication to Leeds

Although I stopped going to away matches for a while whilst I had my first two children, I still carried on going to all the home matches and have done this regardless from then until the present day. I started going to a few away matches again from 1983 and then in 1985 had another seven years of never missing a match home and away. This was when I became secretary of the Selby branch of the Leeds United Supporters Club in 1985 and organised transport and tickets to away matches. I managed to get to all these matches as the family came with me, including Jamie and Michelle who were young at the time. Again whilst running the branch there were only a few women going and football was still dominated by male fans. I didn't like violence and don't condone it because I always ended up being 'targeted' because I wore my colours. There were many times though when you were grateful for our fans being there and sorting things out.

The next generation of Leeds fans were brought up in the only way they could be. I took the kids from being young and brought them up right! You could tell how bad the crowds had got during the 1981–1982 season, because at one match I managed to stand at the back of the Kop with my eldest child whilst heavily pregnant with my second. At the same match Carole had brought a reporter from the *Daily Mail* onto the Kop. Leeds fans had got a bad name at this point for violence at football matches and Carole was trying to show him the good side and what we had to put up with. My son Jamie got a mention in the article as he had been "soothed by the Leeds thugs" when he started to cry. When I started taking the kids to matches on a regular basis, I changed to standing at the front of the Kop with them, only standing at the back if they weren't with me. I took both Jamie and Michelle up to Falkirk for a pre-season friendly with a friend Mike, who took us up in his car. I took a double buggy with me and we managed to get into the seats along with the buggy and two kids (who they let in for free).

I ended up getting married to Phillip (Captain) from Halifax in 1988. I have photos of him in Belgium when we met at Molenbeek, Belgium in a pre-season friendly in 1977 and then met him again when he was running the Halifax Branch of the Leeds United Supporters Club and met at the fortnightly meetings at Leeds in 1986.

Tragedy hit us in 1991 when our beautiful daughter Charlotte died at 17 days old from an undiagnosed heart defect. We were devastated! It was bad enough that we had to go through the trauma but horrendous for Jamie and Michelle. Charlotte in her short life became a star in her own right. Her birth was announced on Sky TV by Greavsie. Leeds were playing down at Arsenal and he announced at half-time that, "Heidi Haigh, a Leeds fan who hasn't missed a match for six years has given birth to a girl. Well Heidi you've seen more action than we have here!" She also attended her first Leeds match against Crystal Palace at six days old and I still think she holds the record to this day. She went in the crèche whilst we watched the match. Before the match we had taken her into the Supporters Club to introduce her to our friends and Marion from London asked what her name was and when I said Charlotte she said what has that got to do with Leeds United?

I carried on running the Supporters Club until the following year even though I'd moved to Halifax in 1988. But the struggle of our trauma plus I was pregnant again meant that I gave up the running of the branch at the end of our promotion winning season 1991–1992. Leeds were crowned champions after our match at Brammall Lane where Leeds won 3–2 with a bizarre own goal and then Liverpool beat man utd at Anfield. Our daughter Danielle ended up being photographed with the cup at five weeks old.

Our youngest daughter Emily has had a season ticket since before she was born in 1993. I was pregnant again and when renewing our season tickets said I wanted to have a season ticket for the baby, although I wasn't due until September. I was told I needed a birth certificate but I said as I was still pregnant that would be a bit difficult! I was given the season ticket so as I said previously she had one before she was born. Danielle (Four) and Emily (two) were also filmed by Sky TV before playing Wimbledon in an evening match at Elland Road. It was great watching the match later as we managed to get in touch with family and asked them to record it for us.

I always wondered what would happen when Billy Bremner (my little hero) left Leeds and the team was broken up, whether I would still follow Leeds. Well the answer is once a Leeds fan, always a Leeds fan. They are forever in your hearts and as I said I am still at Elland Road to this day. It is like my arm is on automatic pilot because whenever I see anyone wearing anything showing they are Leeds fans or have a Leeds sticker in their car, I automatically do the Leeds salute. The salute came in handy many times for Leeds fans to identify themselves without talking, when it was used discreetly if they were in the middle of any trouble. The salute means you chant Leeds, Leeds, Leeds, whilst moving your arm in the direction of your heart at the same time. Which arm you use seems to depend on which hand you write with as I automatically use my right arm. There have been arguments amongst some Leeds fans as to the right way to do the salute, but the left hand obviously does not go over your heart.

We were constantly being called sluts, scrubbers, slags and whores for being female and going to football matches. I still maintain to this day, that there is a difference between going to support your team and sleeping with any Tom, Dick or Harry. We were Leeds through and through and idolised our team, but the thought of sleeping with them didn't even enter our heads. We were totally naïve and always had to defend ourselves. Lads still made their own minds up and thought they had the right to tell us what they thought of us even if they didn't know us.

I feel that the Leeds lads saw me as a challenge and the fact that they thought I'd slept with a Leeds player and not one of them made it even more of a challenge. The truth is I did not sleep with Terry Yorath. I admit I was a flirt and had banter with a lot of our fans in the spirit it was meant to be most of the time (that doesn't mean to say I didn't get upset because I did), but that still doesn't make it wrong. Yes, I got hugged and kissed but that's all it was as I was friendly with all the lads and it was a show of affection. It didn't mean you slept with them. I also had my bum nipped many times, which these days would mean they would get into trouble for sexual harassment, how times change! If I found out that someone actually did fancy me, I used to run away in the opposite direction as I was scared. What I was scared of I don't know and I do think I ran away from the wrong person many a time but unfortunately that is what life is about. You don't always do things that are right and you learn from your experiences.

I also feel in the long run it made me a better person. I do like the good comments as it certainly boosts your ego and makes you feel good but the downside are the bad ones. You are never going to get everyone to agree to the same thing, so as it was you took it on the chin, had a cry, slept on it and the next morning things never looked as bad as they had at the time. I also feel that it did take me a long time to trust anyone and realise that I could enjoy myself. Unfortunately the lads seemed to think I lived it up when I didn't go to watch Leeds but I actually led a very boring life. If Leeds weren't playing I was working, earning money to enable me to go to all the matches and I didn't have a social life unless I stayed at Karens or Caroles at the weekend and went out in Leeds. My life revolved around Leeds United and watching them play football.

Most lads were just talk anyway and you didn't take anything they said seriously if they made passes at you, because most of them already had girlfriends at home anyway. Unfortunately there were a lot of our fans who gave us stick which wasn't nice, but I am still supporting Leeds all these years later although I'm not sure how many of those are still following Leeds. I know a hardcore of them are, because I still see them at matches. Also I didn't realise how violent I sound from reading my memoirs but it goes to show the amount of times we had our bums nipped, suffered from wandering hands or were 'attacked'. The only reason I lashed out was to protect myself, not that it worked though! Although I felt brave against our lads I wouldn't have dared lash out at an opposing fan. Eventually a lot of our fans stopped calling us names once they got to know us better and saw that we were always at the matches. In fact I would say that many of them had a lot of respect for us, so not everything was bad. By having a couple of years away from travelling to the away matches things possibly changed as well, but when I started going back to them it was like I had never been away but without the name calling.

By being a flirt, very vocal and feisty I suppose it gave a wrong impression of me but I would talk to anyone, especially Leeds fans as we all supported the same team and there is nothing wrong with that. Although we had lots of abuse to put up with from some lads, we have made a lot of excellent friends over the years. As I've said before, this is what being a Leeds fan is all about and the cameraderie and friends you have made, means that wherever you go there is always someone you know and we all speak even if you don't see anyone for years. Also in a way, going to football matches and being female was better because when trouble occurred, more often than not we were left alone because of that, whereas the lads ended up with the injuries. Many lads wouldn't hit girls but you always had some who would. We were threatened with rape and called names etc, but not touched apart from times mentioned in the book.

This book is to show what it was like for us girls travelling to see Leeds home and away in the 1970s. The good thing that happened is the fact that we have met loads of people who love our club. I have taken lots of photos of my times following Leeds and I have included a lot in this book, as I feel it is important that they are reflected in my memoirs as proof of where I went. *Follow Me and Leeds United* was one of the stickers I used to have in my car window and a patch on my waistcoat and is what gave me the idea for a book title. Also we had our little gang of lads who used to hero worship us, although we weren't aware of it at the time.

There are so many more tales to tell of different events and I will get together with Carole and Sue and see if we can come up with a load more. The one thing that always does happen when groups of Leeds fans get together from these days, is reminiscing about the times and troubles of following Leeds. There are lots of hilarious and frightening things, but times have really changed and many things that happened in those times would never happen today. I am still at Elland Road at all the home matches and go to some away matches, and I will still be there in years to come.

Marching on Together, We all Love Leeds!!

ND - #0274 - 270225 - C0 - 234/156/14 - PB - 9781780913087 - Gloss Lamination